Time to Rethink Risk Management

Surviving Future Global Crises

Time to Rethink Risk Management
Surviving Future Global Crises

TONY BENDELL

Services Limited, UK & The Anti-Fragility Academy, UK

World Scientific

NEW JERSEY • LONDON • SINGAPORE • BEIJING • SHANGHAI • HONG KONG • TAIPEI • CHENNAI • TOKYO

Published by

World Scientific Publishing Co. Pte. Ltd.
5 Toh Tuck Link, Singapore 596224
USA office: 27 Warren Street, Suite 401-402, Hackensack, NJ 07601
UK office: 57 Shelton Street, Covent Garden, London WC2H 9HE

Library of Congress Control Number: 2023930270

British Library Cataloguing-in-Publication Data
A catalogue record for this book is available from the British Library.

TIME TO RETHINK RISK MANAGEMENT
Surviving Future Global Crises

ISBN 978-981-126-448-1 (hardcover)
ISBN 978-981-126-449-8 (ebook for institutions)
ISBN 978-981-126-450-4 (ebook for individuals)

For any available supplementary material, please visit
https://www.worldscientific.com/worldscibooks/10.1142/13090#t=suppl

Desk Editor: Nicole Ong

Typeset by Stallion Press
Email: enquiries@stallionpress.com

Preface: Setting the Scene

The intent of the Preface of this book is to establish both the current development of Risk Management, with its achievements and limitations, and its specific limitations in the reality of the Global Crises we now face.

The Progress of Risk Management

Risk Management is today a great success, an impressive achievement, and a notable failure. It works, and it doesn't work. It saves lives and property, and it fails to save lives and property. It helps and it hinders. Like all such management approaches, this has a lot to do with how it is employed and practised but, in the case of Risk Management, there is also a much more fundamental issue. The Risk Management framework, the Risk Management model, is wrong.

That should not be a surprise, since at best such management formulations reflect the best current thinking on fundamental issues. With time and experience, these are refined and improved taking us closer to the reality they represent. Only, in this case, this development, this learning, this growth, has perhaps paused. To make real progress with Risk Management, we now need a fundamental rethink, a paradigm shift. The current Risk Management framework has taken us as far as it can, and it's not far enough to meet our current needs.

Why? At the most basic level, part of the problem is the way we define, we think about, Risk. Risk as a concept is a human construct: our way of coping with and trying to predict and manage the unknown. It reflects the fact that 'Organisations of all types and sizes face external and internal factors and influences that make it uncertain whether they will achieve their objectives' (ISO 31000: 2018). *Risk* is then defined as the effect this uncertainty has in relation to the achievement of the organisation's objectives. This view of risk as a human construct is valid, whether or not one believes in a probabilistic, or a deterministic universe.

We will argue below that the way we conceive, and approach, risk and its management has led to increased exposure and fragility, which we can no longer afford. However, until now, often this approach to risk has served the World well despite its serious limitations.

As a result of the spectacular failures of governance, in general terms, regulatory, professional and corporate risk management has been strengthened and progressively improved across many sectors. Risk management has steadily improved in recent years, due to the application of specific learning at the macro/industry-level to improvement at the micro/organisation-level. For example, sectors, such as the airline industry, have applied the lessons learnt from catastrophes to help prevent their reoccurrence in the future.

In addition, bodies like the Health and Safety Executive and the Environment Agency in the UK have progressively applied their global learning in relation to their specialised areas of risk, to reduce individual organisation's risks through education and information. Improvements in Risk Management at the organisational level have been achieved also by the utilisation of global system standards like ISO 14001 for the environment, ISO 45001 for occupational health and safety, as well as ISO 9001 for Quality Management. Within these, there is a requirement for ongoing risk reduction, as well as containment of issues, organisational learning and corrective and preventive action.

The international standard for Risk Management, ISO 31000: 2018, represents the current established 'legitimate' approach to Risk Management and the underlying paradigm. In many senses, it is a good standard, but it suffers from the fundamental weakness that it is based on a human construct, and unless you can conceive of a risk, it will not be included in your Risk Management.

Over the last two decades, the desire for a coherent holistic approach to risk across an organisation has been the basis for the emergence of

Enterprise Risk Management (ERM) as a new management discipline that calls for organisations to identify all the risks they face, to decide which risks to manage actively, and then to make that plan of action available to all stakeholders, rather than just shareholders, as part of their annual reporting. Risk is seen not just as upcoming threats but also in terms of opportunities that may balance them. The release of the Committee of Sponsoring Organizations' (COSO's) ERM Integrated Framework in 2004 did much to establish ERM, and it has now become a business school/MBA discipline.

ERM is generally seen to be a process, ongoing and flowing through an organisation and affected by people at every level within it, which is applied in strategy setting and across the enterprise at every level and unit and includes taking an organisational-level portfolio view of risk. It is designed to identify potential events that, if they occur, will affect the organisation and to manage risk within its risk appetite, so as to be able to provide reasonable assurance to management and the board of directors, geared to the achievement of objectives.

But, ERM also has its shortfalls, including also being based on the human construct. The practical difficulties in applying it also mean that in reality its application is limited to a relatively small number of organisations, with limited risk coverage, limited holistic formulation and limited effectiveness. For example, a Deloitte & Touche survey back in 2005 found that at that time 45% of organisations had no formal ERM programme, while of the remainder, only 49% had a programme in development and only 6% considered ERM fully operational.

It is also commonly acknowledged that while ERM is conceptually relatively straightforward, its implementation is not. This may mean that an organisation's implementation in practice may have limited coverage of risks, particularly qualitative hard to measure ones, too much emphasis just on defensive regulatory compliance and rubberstamping, limited holistic bringing together of risks from the distinct risk silos and limited effectiveness. There may also be blame avoidance, an emphasis on time spent filling forms and ticking appropriate boxes, time spent maximising the achievement of target metrics rather than progressing true objectives, and an emphasis on the wrong risks due to disproportionate regulators' or stakeholders' pressure.

The Phases of Crisis Management

What exactly is a Crisis anyway? According to Wikipedia, a Crisis is as follows:

> *Any event or period that will lead, or may lead, to an unstable and dangerous situation affecting an individual, group, or all of society. Crises are negative changes in the human or environmental affairs, especially when they occur abruptly, with little or no warning.*

In contrast, the Cambridge English Dictionary defines Crisis varyingly as follows:

- *a time of great disagreement, confusion, or suffering*
- *an extremely difficult or dangerous point in a situation*
- *a moment during a serious illness when there is the possibility of suddenly getting either better or worse*

Collins English Dictionary defines a Global Crisis as follows:

- A crisis is a situation in which something or someone is affected by one or more very serious problems.
- You can use global to describe something that happens in all parts of the world or affects all parts of the world.

There are varying classifications of phases within Crises, varying commonly from three to six phases. Generally, though, there is consensus that paraphrasing, a Crisis instigates, happens and is resolved. The phases of Crisis Management vary between authors in how they treat planning and control through this cycle. For our purposes, the details of this is not too important, for instance, if there are six phases rather than three. What is important is that a Crisis by definition has at minimum these three phases, so that, in considering Risk Management in the context of Global Crises, we must differentiate the planning and control activities within these three phases, not treat the Crisis as an instantaneous risk with instantaneous impact.

At all levels, risks need to be managed through the three phases and ignoring the phases negates the management of the risk of Crisis, instead treating it as purely an aggregated chance of disaster with an aggregated response to mitigate or manage its effects. In this way, Risk Management can fail to take account of the way that Global Crises initiate, propagate and dissipate and so becomes inefficient and ineffective.

If, as is often the case, our models of organisational risk management are structured so that they treat systemic risks, the mechanisms of occurrence for big society changing hazards, essentially indifferently from those for the occurrences of routine everyday hazards to the individual organisation, these separate phases are ignored and the corresponding aggregation sacrifices essential information about the mechanism underlying the big hazard's realisation that undermines effective organisational planning and control.

The fact that such an approach is inadequate can be identified easily from the inherent nature of systemic risks like the risk of breakdowns in an entire system, as opposed to breakdowns in individual parts and components. While mainly discussed to date in the context of economic or financial risks, systemic risks, in general, may be characterised by the following:

- modest 'tipping points' combining indirectly to produce large failures,
- 'contagion', as one loss triggers a chain of others,
- 'hysteresis', with systems being unable to recover equilibrium after a shock.

It follows that in our organisational risk management we should instead focus on identifying and monitoring the potential phases of the Crisis, then identifying, monitoring and mitigating the organisational effects of potential tipping points, and identifying, monitoring and mitigating the state of the contagion mechanism and the state of hysteresis.

Managing Through a Global Crisis

Despite the progress of Risk Management, it is not common organisational practice today for organisations to proactively monitor and manage their response to an emerging Crisis, with many organisations only becoming somewhat proactive when sometime after initiation the Crisis enters the propagation or contagion phase. At this point, industry guidance, regulator requirements or government entreaty may precipitate organisational action. Unfortunately, possibly somewhat late, even in high-risk situations.

For example, on March 23rd 2020, Lexology published *Planning in a time of pandemic: Considerations for regulated financial institutions in the US, EU and UK* including the following note:

> **European Union, United Kingdom, USA March 18 2020**
> *The economic and operational stresses caused by the Novel Coronavirus (COVID-19) are highlighting the need for regulated financial institutions to formulate responses to address significant business disruptions (SBDs) and to revisit and enhance their business continuity plans (BCPs). Financial institutions should review and consider their policies in light of the threats posed by SBDs and also consider their obligations under their respective regulatory regimes. In addition to pandemic-specific guidance published by financial regulators in light of COVID-19, the relevant regulatory agencies have also previously published general business continuity guidance which should be followed in these circumstances. For financial institutions operating on a cross-border basis, different responses to the regulatory requirements may be required or otherwise a global policy that covers all elements or the most stringent requirements should be put in place.*
>
> *We have already commented on the position for broker-dealers and now comment more broadly for banks as well as broker-dealers, and on a trans-Atlantic basis. You may also like to see our other client notes relating to the impact of COVID-19, such as the impact for derivatives and the use of force majeure provisions in commercial contracts.*

Indeed, the forms of word above also draw attention to the lack of a holistic risk management approach to managing through the whole Crisis, instead of focusing on the need to do something now at this (late) stage.

The Six Fundamental Truths about Crises

It can be said that there are six fundamental truths about Global Crises. These are as follows:

1. There's going to be another Global Crisis. Do you doubt it? There is, in fact, going to be an ongoing stream of Crises. Why? Because Crises reflect the realisation of systemic risks and arise out of lack of

understanding; human, government and societal complacency; lack of monitoring and awareness; and lack of adequate timely responses. The more joined up is the global community, the greater is the global complexity and connectiveness, then the more the potential is for Crises to be global. So, the occurrence of Global Crises is potentially an escalating phenomenon.

2. The next Global Crisis will not be just Financial or just a pandemic. We mislabel crises. Is a Financial Crisis purely Financial? Surely not, since its initiation, propagation and consequences all have societal elements other than just economic ones. Is the Coronavirus Crisis entirely well named when it has major economic implications and the main determining element in its propagation is not the natural spread of the disease but instead how responding systems and human behaviour affect that and impact personal, organisational, societal and economic survival? In reality, all Global Crises are multidimensional, originating perhaps in part of the sustainability space that is specifically economic, societal or environmental, but then being propagated to crisis point by mechanisms that play out across all spheres of sustainability. A Crisis is, by definition, an impending threat to sustainment.
3. Current Risk Management is fatally flawed. There are numerous repeated and well-publicised failures of Risk Analysis and Management. See, for example, the Roads to Ruin study report from the Cass Business School (Atkins *et al.*, 2011) which identified seven broad residual risk categories from the study of crises affecting 21 organisations. There are many flaws of current Risk Management, including failing to take full account of all aspects of the internal and external conditions in the system or organisation, including its complexity and loading. However, the absolutely fatal issue is that if you can't conceive the risk, then with current Risk Management it is not included in your Risk Assessment. Accordingly, Black Swan events are excluded, and Risk Management in the context of Global Crises is fatally flawed.
4. What we expect often comes to pass. There is a reason for that or rather more than one. It could be that what we expect is likely anyway, that the more likely it is, the more we expect it, so what we expect does often come to pass. This requires our expectations to be reasonable. Alternatively, and relevant in our current context, it may be that our very state of expectation positively influences the probability of occurrence. This is

an illustration of the principle of Expectation Influenced Probability developed by the fantasy author Jasper Fforde. Such a concept, while farfetched for natural phenomena, is fundamentally sound where the event whose probability of occurrence we are considering is strongly influenced by human action, or inaction, such as that occurs in relation to markets or Global Crises.

5. What we don't expect usually doesn't come to pass, until we do expect it to. As a corollary to the previous 'truth', if we expect something not to occur, or equivalently we don't expect it to occur, then it follows from Truth 4 that it often won't. However, it also follows that if we start to expect it to occur, then it often will.
6. It will be different next time. This one is a pretty safe bet too. While there can be much commonality, all aspects of real life, including Global Crises, vary and do not replicate past experiences exactly. This is reinforced by the multidimensional and dynamic nature and complexity of Global Crises. Furthermore, again following the logic of Expectation Influenced Probability, we tend to reduce the likelihood of a pure repeat of a previous crisis by the introduction of remedial preventive safeguards following such a major negative occurrence. So, whatever the next Global Crisis will be, it won't be the same exactly as the last one.

Changing Current Practice

Based on the above discussion, the need for change to current risk management paradigms and practices is obvious, particularly in the context of Global Crises.

As conventionally defined, *Risk* is the effect of uncertainty on the achievement of the organisation's objectives so that Risk Management is perforce reactive to uncertainties, which gives an implied independent variable status for these uncertainties, that is, outside our control, so we can only react. That is the basis of conventional definitions of Risk Management. Such need for reactiveness to unforeseen uncertainties implies fragility, as it will generally require intervention for remedy after the realisation of an uncertain event to contain, mitigate or neutralise its effects. Such reaction may be inadequate, misconceived or too late. Anyway, it implies that we are just waiting for the bad things to happen.

But the Oxford English Dictionary also gives us a useful alternative definition of *Risk*, as well as that of a situation involving exposure to danger and the possibility that something unpleasant or unwelcome will happen. This is taking responsibility for one's own safety or possessions, such as in the phrase *They undertook the adventure at their own risk.*

With this definition of Risk, Risk Management can be much more concerned with proactivity, rather than reactivity, and becomes less a checking and controlling process and more a movement towards system design for prevention and anti-fragility. This proactivity is needed in the context of Global Crises; we should not be waiting for the bad things to happen and then reacting. We should be fully prepared and aware. Unfortunately, the inherent nature of Global Crises is that we are not.

The purpose of this book is to change thinking about Crises and Risk. The author believes that Risk Management has come a long way, but that evidence of its more recent failure is now all around us and that it needs to now change dramatically if it is to accommodate current realities. The book is also based on the view that while there is a clear need for us all to manage Risk through a Crisis, there is a lack of understanding of the nature of Crises that is impeding progress.

As well as providing a conceptual basis for changing the way Risk Management is undertaken, the book provides a blueprint for managing at the organisational level through a global crisis, as well as providing some insights at national and global levels; how to prepare, what to do when it's happening and how and when to emerge into the post-crisis world.

Contents

1

A Model of Global Crises and a Consequential Model for ERM

Introduction

As we said in the Preface, there are varying classifications of phases within Crises, varying commonly from three to six phases. Generally, though, there is consensus that, paraphrasing, a Crisis instigates, happens and is resolved.

In Chapter 1 we discuss the nature of Global Crises and how they arise, develop and discharge. We establish their multidimensional characteristics, key phases and mechanisms. Developing causal models for their occurrence, we identify the required differences in risk management needed given the distinct phases and we explore the implications for appropriate Enterprise Risk Management within organisations.

We start with instigation. From much earlier usage, the concept of Black Swans came into prominence in the context of the 2007–2008 Global Financial Crisis. A Black Swan is a rare unpredictable high-impact event. In his 2007 book *The Black Swan: The Impact of the Highly Improbable*, Nassim Nicholas Taleb defines a Black Swan Event as follows:

> *A black swan is a highly improbable event with three principal characteristics: it is unpredictable; it carries a massive impact; and, after the fact, we concoct an explanation that makes it appear less random, and more predictable, than it was.*

It would be nice to think that Global Crises are always instigated by genuine Black Swans as, if not, some national, international or organisational authority should have foreseen their occurrence and taken appropriate steps, instigating highly effective safeguards and/or emergency arrangements for when the Black Swan occurs. Instead, with Global Crises, all players are typically playing 'catch up', with too little, and not always appropriate, action, too late.

Initiating Sequences and Events; Black, Grey and White Swans

In reality, in most cases, it is extremely difficult to argue that a Global Crisis has been instigated by a Black Swan. For example, amongst others, Nassim Nicholas Taleb argues that the current Coronavirus Crisis is very much a White Swan. A definition for these is as follows:

> *A white swan is a highly certain event with three principal characteristics: it is certain; it carries an impact that can easily be estimated; and, after the fact, we concoct an explanation that recognises the certainty of occurrence, but again, shifts the focus to errors in judgment or some other human form of causation.*

In between the Black and White Swans are Grey Swans[1]:

> *A grey swan is a highly probable event with three principal characteristics: it is predictable; it carries an impact that can easily cascade; and, after the fact, we concoct an explanation that recognises the probability of occurrence, but shifts the focus to errors in judgment or some other human form of causation.*

It follows that, in general, Global Crises will initiate from the occurrence of Black, White or Grey Swan events. While Black Swans are defined as entirely unexpected events, White Swans are entirely expected events and Grey Swans are in between the two. The argument as to what colour of Swan is associated with the initiation of any specific Global Crisis

[1] See https://accendoreliability.com/black-swans-grey-swans-white-swans/.

is of great importance since it defines the level of premonition of upcoming crisis and possible safeguards and mitigation that could be expected to, or aspired to, be in place.

As we will see in Chapter 2, even with Black Swans, it is not unreasonable to expect, or even to legislate for, basic safeguards against the occurrence of the undesired initiating sequence or event. Such 'Precautionary Principles' are fundamental to human thinking, whether the issue or risk is recognised or not.

For example, in environmental law and sustainability, we typically try to employ this concept as a strategy for approaching issues of potential harm when extensive scientific knowledge on the matter is lacking. It emphasises caution, pausing and review before leaping into new innovations that may prove disastrous.

Of course, critics argue that this is unscientific and an obstacle to progress and, with minor exceptions, Precautionary Principles have not been well discussed in the broader context. One such exception arising from the 2007–2008 Financial Crisis is the precautionary principle that Board members of organisations should always have *skin in the game.*

But since, in reality, Global Crises arise often, and arguably typically, from Grey or White Swans, which by definition are predictable, it follows that a much higher level of awareness and foresight, together with deployed safeguards and emergency arrangements, should be possible.

Furthermore, since Global Crises are by definition threats to the sustainment of the global order and system, it follows that the initiating event may be in any part of the Economic, Societal and Environmental Sustainability Space.

Indeed, we frequently mislabel crises. Is a Financial Crisis purely Financial? Surely not, since its initiation, propagation and consequences all have societal elements other than just economic ones. Is the COVID-19 Crisis entirely well named when it has major economic implications and the main determining element in its propagation is not the natural spread of the disease but instead how responding human behaviour affects that and impacts personal, organisational, societal and economic survival?

In reality, all Global Crises are multidimensional, originating perhaps in part of the sustainability space that is specifically economic, societal or environmental but then being propagated to crisis point by mechanisms that play out across all the three spheres of sustainability.

Whether Global Crises are initiated by an initiating event or an initiating sequence is, perhaps, an academic point. As we discussed in the Preface, with systemic risks once an initiating event occurs, a sequence unravels whereby modest 'tipping points' combine indirectly to produce large failures, 'contagion' occurs as one loss triggers a chain of others and then 'hysteresis' occurs, with systems being unable to recover equilibrium after a shock.

Following the initiating event, or at the end of this initiation sequence, the Crisis has reached such a magnitude that its impending threat is now substantially visible, and it now progresses further to unfold to Crisis Point, when the anticipated maximum danger, damage and threat are realised.

Exponential and Logistic Growth

As we have discussed above, the mechanisms driving the emerging Crisis to crisis point are multidimensional across the Sustainability Space. But, how does the Crisis propagate itself from visibility to Crisis Point?

It is common when discussing Global Crises to talk in terms of exponential growth. For the current Coronavirus Crisis, Google, for example, identifies over four million such references (Figure 1.1).

But, the identification of exponential growth of a Crisis is not specific to an epidemic or pandemic and Google provides some twelve and a half million sources for *exponential growth of crisis* (Figure 1.2).

As well as having empirical support, the argument for exponential growth from emergence to Crisis Point is essentially based on the rate of spread of the Crisis being proportional to its current size. So, early on growth seems slow, but it becomes quicker and quicker, as in Figure 1.3.

A mechanism to explain this in an epidemic is obvious; the more of the population who are infected, the greater the risk of infection to the rest of the population.

Outside of epidemics, a similar focus on relationships between members of the population provides explanatory models for exponential growth. For example, the greater the default on debt, the greater the rate of increase of default on debt, as debtors may have no choice but to default on debt themselves, or even, the greater the level of debt, then the greater the rate of increase of debt.

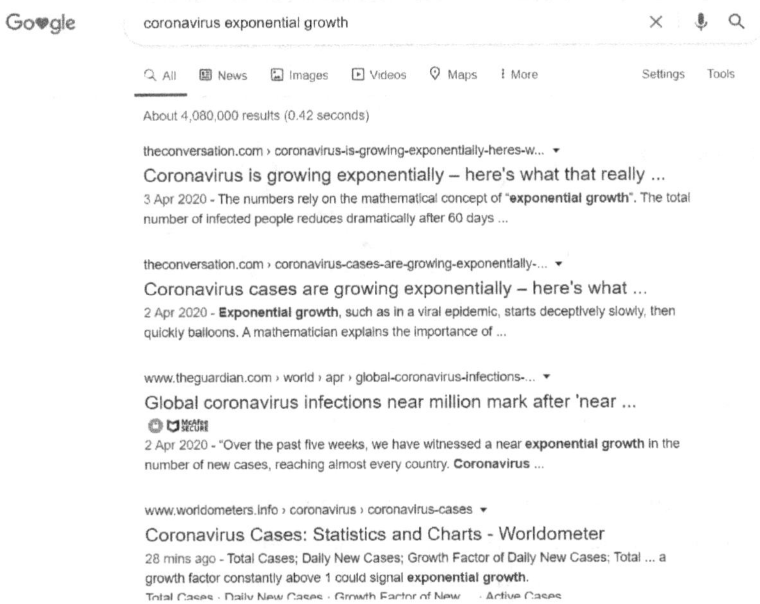
Google
coronavirus exponential growth
All News Images Videos Maps More Settings Tools
About 4,080,000 results (0.42 seconds)

theconversation.com › coronavirus-is-growing-exponentially-heres-w...
Coronavirus is growing exponentially – here's what that really ...
3 Apr 2020 - The numbers rely on the mathematical concept of "**exponential growth**". The total number of infected people reduces dramatically after 60 days ...

theconversation.com › coronavirus-cases-are-growing-exponentially-...
Coronavirus cases are growing exponentially – here's what ...
2 Apr 2020 - **Exponential growth**, such as in a viral epidemic, starts deceptively slowly, then quickly balloons. A mathematician explains the importance of ...

www.theguardian.com › world › apr › global-coronavirus-infections-...
Global coronavirus infections near million mark after 'near ...
2 Apr 2020 - "Over the past five weeks, we have witnessed a near **exponential growth** in the number of new cases, reaching almost every country. **Coronavirus** ...

www.worldometers.info › coronavirus › coronavirus-cases
Coronavirus Cases: Statistics and Charts - Worldometer
28 mins ago - Total Cases; Daily New Cases; Growth Factor of Daily New Cases; Total ... a growth factor constantly above 1 could signal **exponential growth**.

Figure 1.1. Extract from Google for 'Coronavirus Exponential Growth' in May 2020

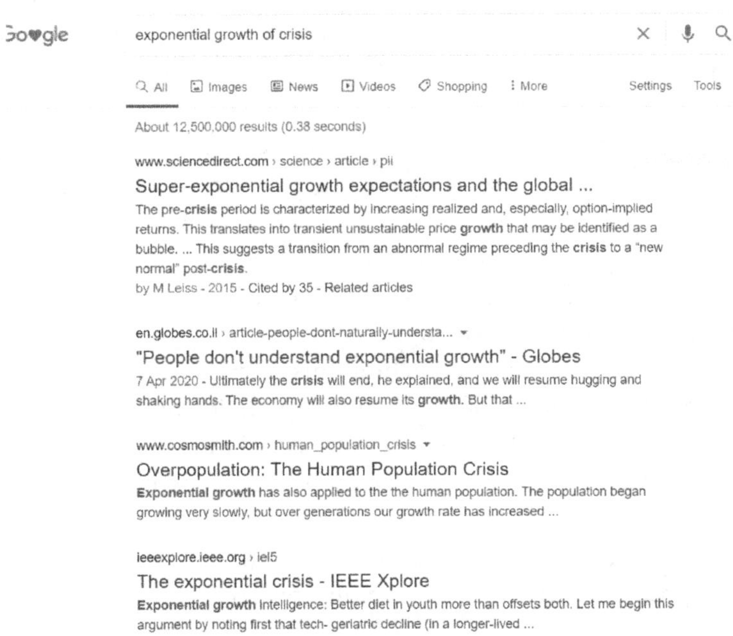
Google
exponential growth of crisis
All Images News Videos Shopping More Settings Tools
About 12,500,000 results (0.38 seconds)

www.sciencedirect.com › science › article › pii
Super-exponential growth expectations and the global ...
The pre-**crisis** period is characterized by increasing realized and, especially, option-implied returns. This translates into transient unsustainable price **growth** that may be identified as a bubble. ... This suggests a transition from an abnormal regime preceding the **crisis** to a "new normal" post-**crisis**.
by M Leiss - 2015 - Cited by 35 - Related articles

en.globes.co.il › article-people-dont-naturally-understa...
"People don't understand exponential growth" - Globes
7 Apr 2020 - Ultimately the **crisis** will end, he explained, and we will resume hugging and shaking hands. The economy will also resume its **growth**. But that ...

www.cosmosmith.com › human_population_crisis
Overpopulation: The Human Population Crisis
Exponential growth has also applied to the the human population. The population began growing very slowly, but over generations our growth rate has increased ...

ieeexplore.ieee.org › iel5
The exponential crisis - IEEE Xplore
Exponential growth intelligence: Better diet in youth more than offsets both. Let me begin this argument by noting first that tech- geriatric decline (in a longer-lived ...

Figure 1.2. Extract from Google for 'Exponential Growth of Crisis' in May 2020

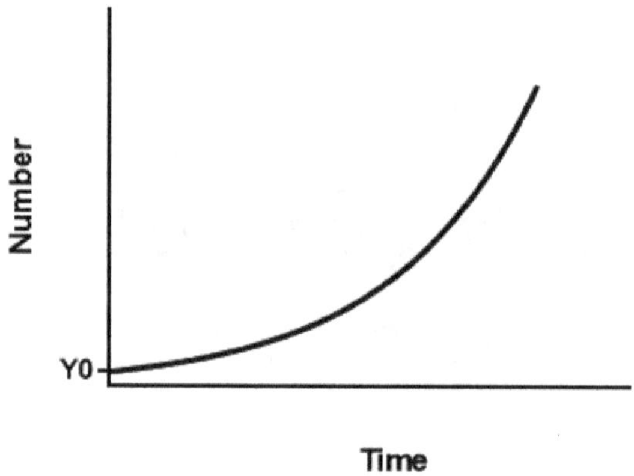

Figure 1.3 Exponential Growth Curve

Thus, in this exponential growth, human behaviour and underlying assumptions, values and beliefs are fundamental to the underlying mechanisms of propagation. And underlying this is human expectation, since our attitude to risk acceptance is determined by our belief in whether the hazard will actually materialise. We shall return to this argument.

In some Crises, there is an ongoing exponential growth towards a Crisis Point, where the *fat hits the pan* and new or novel measures or remedies are then introduced to deal with it, often point events, such as suspension of trading.

However, in others, the propagating force of exponential growth begins to be balanced, at first gradually, by counter pressures, as the exponential growth directly causes a balancing effect. This results in the upwards exponential curve beginning to curve downwards from an 'inflection point', resulting in an S-shaped logistic growth curve rather than the ever-upwards exponential curve. See Figure 1.4.

In epidemics, the mechanism behind this transition from exponential growth to logistic growth is often the finite limitations of the population meaning that after a time there are fewer potential individuals to be newly infected, an inadequate number to sustain the rate of infection.

In other Crises, the logistic growth curve is created because the Crisis growth rate decreases as it approaches the maximum size of the Crisis possible imposed by external constraints, referred to as the Carrying

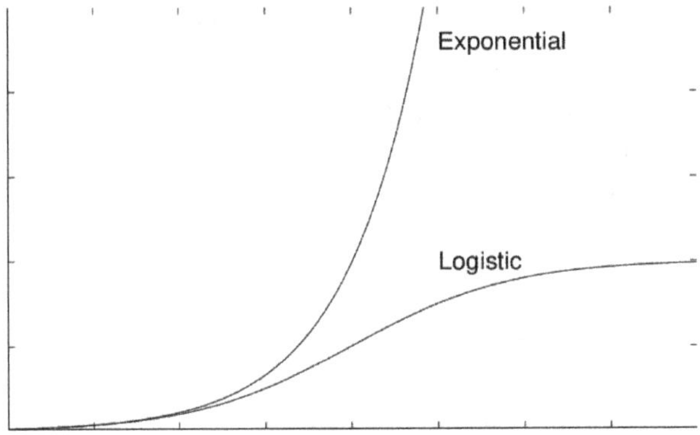

Figure 1.4. Exponential and Logistic Growth

Capacity. An example is financial crises with stock market bubbles and crashes, where there is a limit on capital accumulation.

Soft Systems Thinking

It is in the nature of Global Crises that they exhibit some complexity: complexity associated with the perspectives and behaviours of human beings, such as 'bandwagon effects'.

As communication and connectivity have increased with the help of technology, the potential for initiation and rapid escalation to Crisis Point has also increased. The more joined up is the global community, the greater is the global complexity and connectiveness, then the more the potential is for Crises to be global. So, the occurrence of Global Crises is potentially an escalating phenomenon.

Furthermore, since all Global Crises are multidimensional, perhaps originating in part of the sustainability space that is specifically economic, societal or environmental, but then being propagated to crisis point by mechanisms that play out across all the three spheres of sustainability, it follows that how a specific Crisis will play out is complex. A potentially insignificant occurrence in one domain or sphere may instigate, or contribute to, the emergence or realisation of a systemic risk that may trigger a Global Crisis.

In such circumstances, a good representation of the mechanisms behind a Crisis can be provided by the use of Soft Systems Thinking. This is because Soft Systems Thinking can provide considerable insight into the working of mechanisms within human society.

Soft Systems Thinking is useful in the context of systems involving human beings, where to understand what is happening we need to consider the often conflicting behaviours and perspectives (or holons) of those involved. It is focused on the complexity, causality and mutual interdependence that exists amongst many variables. Rather than postulating structure and dissecting the elements of the human system, which is the approach of Hard System models, instead Soft Systems Thinking focuses on the total linked systems and takes a universal view.

To understand the nature of Soft System Thinking, one needs to understand its partial origins from within the Hard Systems Thinking world. This is the world of Systems Analysis, Management Science, Structured Methods and Operations Research. Typically, such Hard Systems approaches assume that the problems associated with systems are well defined and have a single optimum solution, and that a scientific approach to problem solving will work well, and technical factors will tend to predominate.

During the 1970s, the effectiveness of the Hard Approaches was seriously challenged. The failure of Management Science and Operational Research was strongly debated by various authors including Churchman and Ackoff in the US and Checkland in the UK. The basis of the argument was that in situations in which the problem is not well defined, the Hard Approaches did not offer a suitable methodology. The Hard Approach works well when the problem and objectives we want to achieve were well defined, but in situations when the 'problem' itself is not clear, the Hard Approaches fail to give useful insights.

Peter Checkland argues that this is mainly because these approaches see the situation as an engineering problem, looking at 'how to do things' when 'what to do' is already defined. Thus, when these methods were applied in social systems, for example, to the public sector in California State in the early 1960s, the results were disappointing.

Thus, the Soft Systems Methodology (SSM) had been developed in England by academics at the University of Lancaster Systems Department led by Professor Checkland, through a 10-year action research programme around the late 1960s. It was seen as an approach to organisational process modelling or business process modelling that can be used both for general problem solving and in the management of change.

A particular consideration in our context of the mechanisms behind Global Crises is the distinction commonly made between the characteristics of human-made systems and natural systems. Natural systems, such as a living body or an ecosystem such as a meadow, have an enormous number and complexity of components and interactions, with virtually an infinite number of connections to all systems around them. In contrast, human-made systems, such as motor cars, can still be quite complex, but typically not quite as much, and are not as intricately linked to the systems around them. Thus, human-made systems are more self-contained and less open than natural systems.

But what about human organisations and society? It is reasonable to argue that these exhibit something of a mixture between the characteristics of human-made and natural systems: the formal or 'hard' part of the organisation or society — legal and constitutional systems, organisational structures, governance rules, management, skills, processes, procedures and technology-based systems — behaving in isolation like human-made systems, but the informal or 'soft' aspect of the organisation — the culture, leadership, team working, motivation and sense of 'ownership' — being like natural systems.

When combined holistically within a human organisation or society, the resulting complexity means that any attempt to analyse the organisation's or society's behaviour and performance on a 'hard' basis is only, at best, naïve and likely to lead to very wrong outcomes. It also means that the sources of fragility and anti-fragility within the organisation and society arise both within, and between, the 'hard' and 'soft' aspects.

This fits with the practical experience that the people aspects of organisations and societies can be both their greatest strengths and their greatest weaknesses, and that in implementing organisational or societal change, we need to work holistically on both systems and cultural aspects. Being a 'toolhead' alone is not enough!

A further key to using Soft Systems Thinking to study the mechanisms behind Global Crises is to consider the generally agreed defining characteristics of such systems. These are the following:

1. For a system to carry out its purpose optimally, all the system's parts must be present.
2. These parts must be arranged in a specific way for the system to carry out its purpose.
3. All systems have specific purposes within larger systems.
4. Systems maintain their own stability through fluctuations and adjustments.
5. Systems have feedback.

Apart from the loss of optimal functionality, at the most basic, something missing in a system, organisation or society typically may cause fragility and the inability to cope in extreme conditions. This is because if we can take away parts of the system, organisation or society without affecting functioning and relationships, then there are few interrelationships between components, so it is more of a collection of parts rather than an organisation or system. Such missing components may include leadership, skills, motivation, a positive culture, planning or control processes, key personnel, role descriptions, instructions and procedures.

However, as part of the use of feedback to maintain the system's, organisation's or society's stability, the system, organisation or society may restructure itself to compensate for the missing parts. Frequently, this will be through compensatory arrangements put in place and undertaken by the human (soft) elements rather than through prior defined (hard) systems, governance rules or processes. These may take time to mobilise under crisis conditions.

A system, human organisation or society in which the parts are not properly arranged for the intended purposes will, if it functions satisfactorily at all, typically exhibit fragility in extreme conditions, as parts and linkages will be compensating for the misalignment and this may break down over time.

Similarly, since all systems have specific purposes within the larger systems in which they are embedded, then in trying to force two systems, organisations or societies together to become a larger one, for example, following an organisational merger or acquisition at the organisational level, or as a result of globalisation at the society level, even if we achieve functionality against purpose, we may create fragility.

Equivalently, subdividing an organisation, system or society does not typically deliver two identical functioning systems, and, if it does, they may well be fragile. Clearly, dividing an elephant in half does not normally give you two identical but smaller elephants, and unfortunately, they are likely to die.

In all of these cases concerned with the arrangement of parts or meeting the system's specific purpose, the human role in compensating in real time for the fragility created is paramount, and, typically at a level of sophistication above that which can be achieved through the 'hard' aspects of the systems. There are various levels of contribution within this role, from operational managers making day-to-day decisions as change occurs to political leaders, executives and specialist change managers who plan and control both day-to-day operations and transitions.

Anyone who has ever been involved in the change process within organisations or society is aware that whatever positive changes you attempt to make to the organisation or society to make it more fit for the future, typically the organisation or society itself in some way appears to resist the changes. This is often blamed on the people, but it is in reality more complicated than that.

Left to themselves, systems maintain their stability, for example, your body seeks to maintain your body temperature around 98.6 degrees Fahrenheit or a company's infrastructure attempts to maintain its designated profit margin.

This tendency for the system, organisation or society to hold steady overall arises because other parts of the system are designed to resist the change you are attempting to make and bring the system's performance back to where it was designed to be. It is achieved through continual interactions, feedback and adjustments within the system and between it and its environment. One may be put in mind of the role of the Oracle in The Matrix films.

This stabilising effect can help restore 'business as usual' after a major system disruption, such as a Global Crisis, but it can also prevent or reduce the effectiveness of needed intervention under crisis conditions. It can also prevent earlier process change or improvement to mitigate an as yet unrealised hazard.

This tendency towards 'Balancing' or resisting change is in a sense the opposite of the Vicious or Virtuous circles that can Reinforce change.

The exponential growth of a Global Crisis reflects a Vicious Circle, while logistic growth also incorporates a subsequent Balancing effect.

Feedback is the mechanism through which information is transmitted through the system, acting as a catalyst for a change in system behaviour, such as when balancing effects come into play to turn exponential growth of a Crisis into logistic growth.

There is both internal feedback and feedback between the system itself and larger systems. This may be slow or quick, and go by multiple varying routings.

The availability and quality of correct timely information, speed of information flow and the ability to properly utilise the information for decision-making, are all key aspects that help define the level of feedback and have a major impact on the escalation of a Crisis to Crisis Point.

Since Global Crises, as well as real managerial problems within organisations, are typically characterised by a web of interconnected circular relationships, Soft Systems Thinking gives us a language to understand and communicate these problems.

In general, Soft Systems Thinking considers the Big Picture rather than the single occurrence or local pattern, it balances the short-term and long-term perspectives, recognises the dynamic, complex and interdependent nature of systems, takes into account both measurable and non-measurable factors, and recognises that we are part of the systems in which we function and that we each influence the systems, as well as being influenced by them.

Considering the Big Picture asks the questions:

- Apart from the obvious explanation for the problem, what other causal explanations could there be?
- Who are the actors in the story?
- What are the linkages between variables?
- How can we expand the Picture to include more actors, variables and linkages?

The need to consider the Big Picture arises because there is a natural tendency, under stress, such as in an emerging Global Crisis, to focus on the immediate, most pressing challenges, not to raise one's head sufficiently to identify the systemic issue but instead to focus on its local immediate realisation. The implication of this is that one is likely to miss

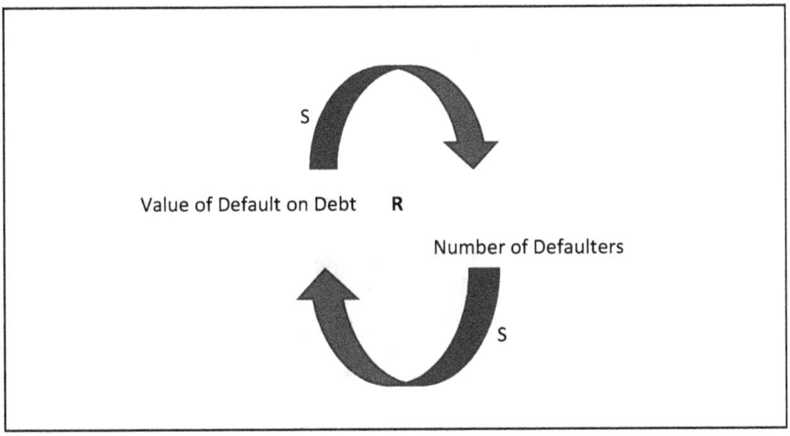

Figure 1.5. A Simple Reinforcing Loop

Source: The Anti-Fragility Academy.

key characteristics of the typically complex problem that really underlies the situation and is, therefore, likely to make incorrect decisions.

Thus, within organisations, management's emphasis tends to be on decomposition of challenges and narrow focus so that they only see the effects of changes elsewhere in system, without appreciating real causes, upcoming further developments and potential risks. In reality, today's problem is part of the bigger picture, and we need to widen the focus to understand the underlying source of the problem to find more effective robust solutions.

The emergence, propagation to Crisis Point and eventual resolution of a Global Crisis can all be described and modelled by considering the Big Picture together with the use of Reinforcing and Balancing Feedback Loops.

These are closed circuits of interconnection between variables, which give sequences of mutual cause and effect. Every feedback loop depicts either a reinforcing process or a balancing process, which is the building block of any dynamic system structure. These can be combined in an infinite variety of ways to produce the complex causal systems that we find around us in practice.

The above Causal Loop Diagram (Figure 1.5) illustrates the simplest possible reinforcing loop: one with just two variables. Here, these are predefined as 'Value of Default on Debt' and the 'Number of Defaulters'.

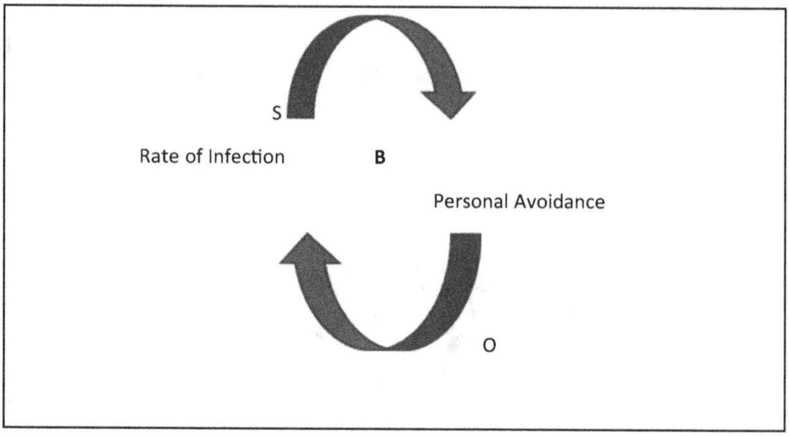

Figure 1.6. A Simple Balancing Loop
Source: The Anti-Fragility Academy.

The 'R' indicates that it is a Reinforcing Loop, and the 'Ss' indicate that both of these relationships have been assumed to work in the same direction, that is, that as the 'Value of Default on Debt' goes up (or down), the 'Number of Defaulters' also goes up or down with it. The relationship between the two variables works the other way round too; as the 'Number of Defaulters' goes up (or down), 'Value of Default on Debt' goes up or down with it. This clearly forms the basis for a Vicious or Virtuous circle, the choice depending only on whether either variable independently starts to get worse or better.

In a similar way, the above Causal Loop Diagram (Figure 1.6) represents the simplest possible balancing loop again one with just two variables: 'Rate of Infection' and 'Personal avoidance'. Here, the 'B' indicates that it is a balancing loop, and this is achieved by the combination of one 'S' link and one 'O' link, the latter indicating an opposite direction relationship so that Rate of Infection declines as Personal Avoidance rises. In this case, we will approach stability, as any rise (or fall) in Personal Avoidance will result in a fall (or rise) in Rate of Infection, which will then cause a corresponding fall (or rise) in Personal Avoidance, taking us back to where we were.

As discussed above, we can combine such reinforcing and balancing loops in an infinite variety of ways to model the complex systems that we find around us in practice. A simple example is shown in the following:

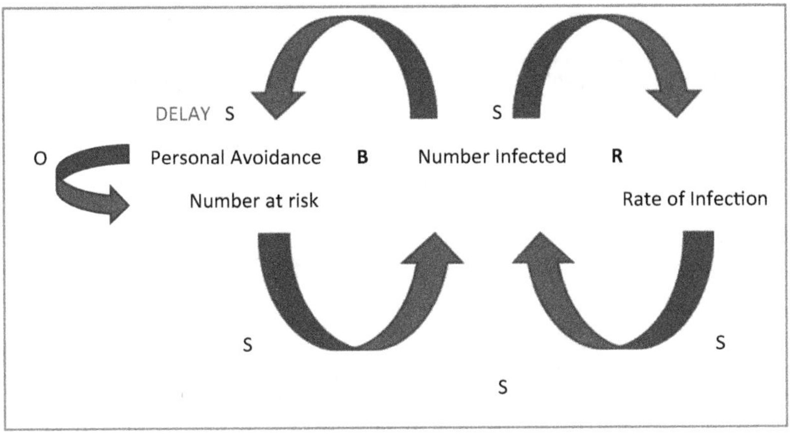

Figure 1.7. Reinforcing and Balancing Loops
Source: The Anti-Fragility Academy.

If we start with a simple Reinforcing Loop for 'Number infected' and 'Rate of infection', which would give us exponential growth as a Viscous Circle, then, perhaps after a delay, we may come to a point where many of the population start to practice Personal Avoidance so that the rate of infection now starts to decline. So, we have added a second, balancing, loop to illustrate this in Figure 1.7.

We can now contrast the Behaviour Over Time (BOT) graphs corresponding to this more complex situation in Figure 1.7, with that for the simple Reinforcing Loop in Figure 1.5. Considering Figure 1.8, we can see that, the two graphs, respectively, correspond to the Logistic and Exponential growths that we discussed previously.

To summarise our discussion of Causal Loop Diagrams, Reinforcing loops are the engines of growth and collapse. They accelerate movement in a given direction and produce Virtuous or Vicious Circles. Sometimes you can spot reinforcing loops are present because you can observe exponential growth or collapse, or from a BOT graph. If there is an even number of 'Os' in a Causal Loop Diagram, or none, then the loop is Reinforcing.

In contrast, Balancing Loops are the great stabilisers, which are generally stabilising or goal seeking. They try to bring things to a desired state and keep them there. They resist change in one direction by producing change in the opposite direction. There is always an inherent visible or

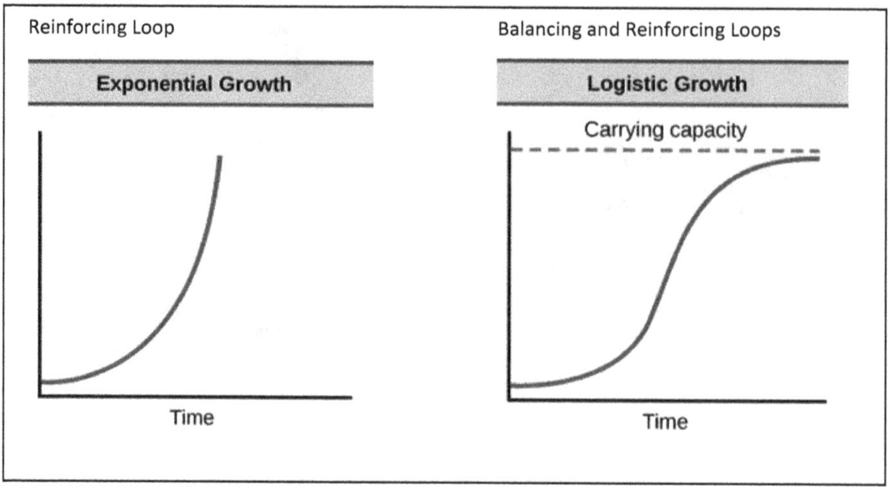

Figure 1.8. Behaviour Over Time Graphs (BOTs)
Source: The Anti-Fragility Academy.

invisible goal in a balancing process, and a Balancing Loop driven by the gap between the goal or desired level and the actual level; as the discrepancy increases, this makes corrective action to reduce the gap.

To detect a Balancing Loop, we need to identify goal-seeking behaviour that characterises a balancing process. For these, conditions keep coming back to some sort of 'norm', no matter what anyone does, the conditions seem to resist change, growth falters or never quite starts, or unproductive behaviour never gets dropped. An odd number of 'Os' indicates a Balancing Loop.

Reinforcing and Balancing Loops combined form the building blocks of complex behaviour; all dynamic behaviour is produced by a combination of Reinforcing and Balancing Loops. Behind any growth or collapse is at least one Reinforcing Loop. For every sign of goal-seeking, there is a Balancing Loop. A period of rapid growth or collapse followed by a slowdown typically signals a shift in dominance from a Reinforcing Loop that is driving the structure to a Balancing Loop.

Delays may occur in these loops. Sometimes there is a misconception, and we fail to take account of them at all. Also, in a Crisis, it often takes too long to perceive feedback, measure results, decide how to respond and implement solutions. This makes the system's behaviour unpredictable.

When considering Global Crises, rather than our above simple examples, these typically include many variables, with many factors at play, and many semi-independent but interlocking components. There is thus a vast number of Reinforcing and Balancing Loops and complicated interconnections. Typically, over time the dominance of different feedback loops shifts, and timing and length of delays vary. Indeed, structures may even seem to be in conflict.

An example representation of the Financial Crisis taken from A Systems View of The Economic Crisis by David Peter Stroh[2] is shown in Figure 1.9.

Such complex systems

- tend to be self-stabilising;
- are, or seem to be, purposeful;
- like simple systems, are capable of using feedback to modify their behaviour;
- can even modify their environments;
- are capable of replicating, maintaining, repairing and reorganising themselves.

The self-stabilising phenomena arise since a complex system, such as a Global Crisis, is likely to contain many Balancing Loops — these each keep some small component of the system in balance or functioning close to some 'desired' level. This creates a relentlessness or resistance to change or attempts at control. Despite intervention, remedial progress falters and propagation of the Crisis returns to its status quo — all the Balancing Loops keep things the way 'the system originally intended' them to be.

The apparent purposefulness occurs as the Balancing Loops seek to maintain the desired level of performance or goal, while the Reinforcing Loops seek to augment or diminish some phenomena in the system. In a complex system, such as an organisation, society or even a Crisis, sometimes the goals of both growth and balancing processes are explicit and known. But often they are contradictory, ambiguous or implicit, and the system appears to function with a mind of its own.

[2] https://thesystemsthinker.com/a-systems-view-of-the-economic-crisis/

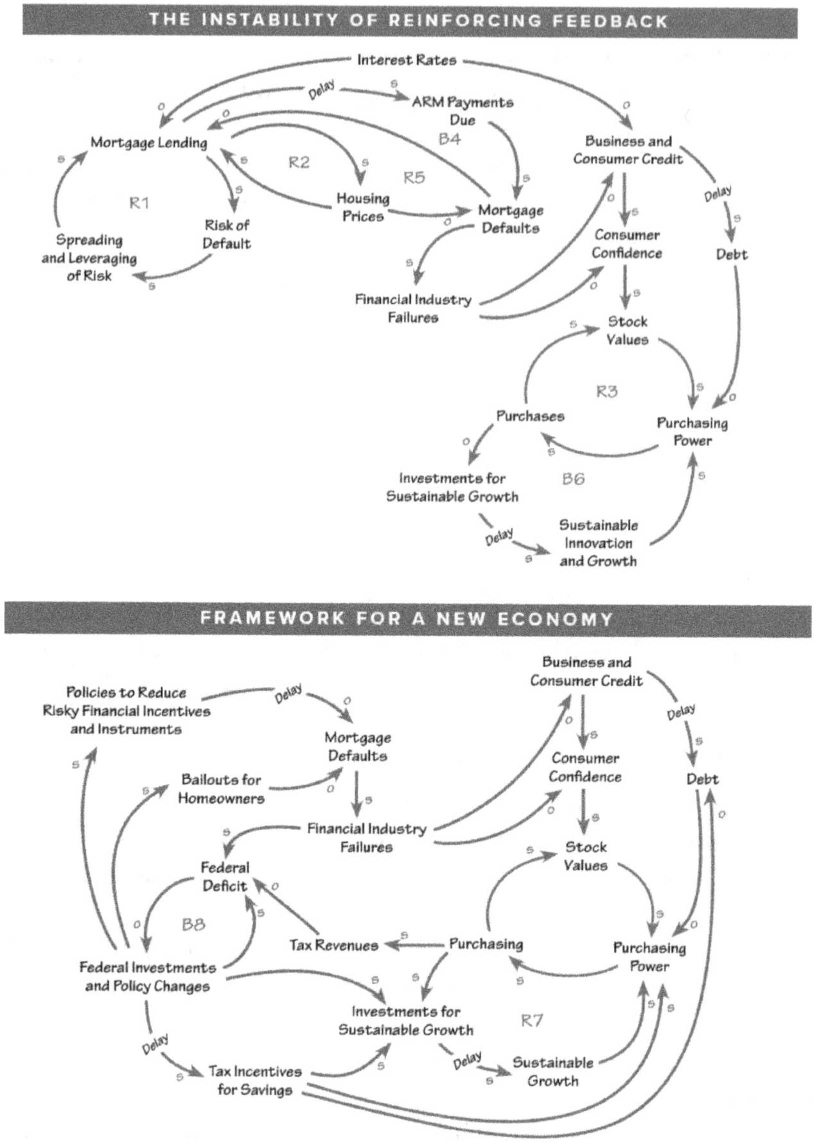

Figure 1.9. Causal Loop Diagram

Using feedback to self-modify behaviour is something all systems, including Global Crises, do. For example, as consumer behaviour changes because of a Financial Crisis, the speed of the Crisis slows down or accelerates accordingly. This provides an opportunity for us to intervene to create change within the system, as a good understanding of the structure and workings of a Crisis help us to take advantage of this to catalyse positive change.

Since complex systems are 'purposeful' and can modify their behaviour, it is not surprising that they can also modify their broader environments. Such modifications may be subtle or bold. Identifying the complex links between the system and its environment helps us to anticipate how changes in the system will lead to changes in the environment.

Crises can replicate themselves, for example, in different localities or repeatedly and chronically. However, as they also change in response to the environment, even apparent clone Crises are likely to contain some unique quirks or mutations. Crises that are abruptly altered, for example, by concerted government intervention, often 'find ways to carry on'. All natural systems can invent, reframe, learn and adjust to their environments, and so can Crises.

The inherent flexibility and looseness of large complex systems, such as some Crises, help them to endure, and because of these features, it may be hard to predict what they do next. The more complex a system is, the greater its potential to process large amounts of information, 'learn' quickly and act flexibly.

On the other side of the equation, the human systems responding to a Global Crisis typically have many subsystems to coordinate, so there is a great potential for things to go wrong. There are many common problems and sources of fragility with such complex systems and organisations. These may develop internally conflicting goals, where the goals of subsystems conflict with system goals, for example, internal politics and empire-ism, and the centralisation/decentralisation dilemma. There may also be distorted feedback, as feedback from local to larger subsystems may be inaccurately conveyed or interpreted. Because of the complexity, there may also be a loss of predictability.

Donella Meadows provided an insightful overall hierarchy of the effectiveness of the types of interventions we can make in intervening in a system, be it an organisation or a Global Crisis. This is shown below, with the lowest effectiveness at the top.

Donella Meadows's 12 leverage points for intervening in a system, in increasing order of effectiveness

12. **Constants, parameters, numbers** (such as subsidies, taxes, and standards).
11. The **size of buffers and other stabilising stocks**, relative to their flows.
10. The **structure of material stocks and flows** (such as transport network and population age structures).
9. The **length of delays**, relative to the rate of system changes.
8. The **strength of negative feedback loops**, relative to the effect they are trying to correct against.
7. The **gain around driving positive feedback loops**.
6. The **structure of information flow** (who does and does not have access to what kinds of information).
5. The **rules of the system** (e.g., incentives, punishments, and constraints).
4. The **power to add, change, evolve or self-organise system structure**.
3. The **goal of the system**.
2. The **mindset or paradigm** that the system, i.e., its goals, structure, rules, delays, and parameters, arises out of.
1. The **power to transcend paradigms**.

Expectation Influenced Probability

Whilst Soft Systems Thinking gives us a language and approach for modelling and responding to the complexity of Global Crises, it in itself does not explain the large impact of human behaviour, such as 'Bandwagon' effects, in causing and propagating the Crisis.

Nor does it account for the related weaknesses inherent in the practice of Risk Management and Business Continuity that we have begun to discuss already in the Preface.

In order to adequately address these human dimensions of Global Crises, it is necessary to introduce a further concept, that of Expectation

Influenced Probability, due to the Fantasy Author, Jasper Fforde in his book *One of Our Thursdays is Missing.* Expectation Influenced Probability is a concept whereby human belief in the occurrence of an upcoming point event influences the probability with which that event will, or will not, occur.

This definition is in contrast to both the current common definitions of Probability: the Classical and the Bayesian views. Essentially, Bayesian statistics defines Probability as a **degree of belief**, while classical statistics defines it as a long-run **relative frequency of occurrence**. Under Bayesian thinking, probability is interpreted as a reasonable expectation representing a state of knowledge or as a quantification of a personal belief.

Expectation Influenced Probability combines aspects of these two views and focuses on **linking the relative frequency of occurrence, or probability, to the degree of belief**. What is interesting is that while, apart from an event I organised with Jasper at the Royal Statistical Society in London, such a concept has had very little attention in the statistical community, the widespread reality of this concept is overwhelmingly apparent in all systems containing human elements and, in consequence, behaviour. Furthermore, this phenomenon can provide a transparent mechanism whereby Global Crises are typically propagated, grown and resolved.

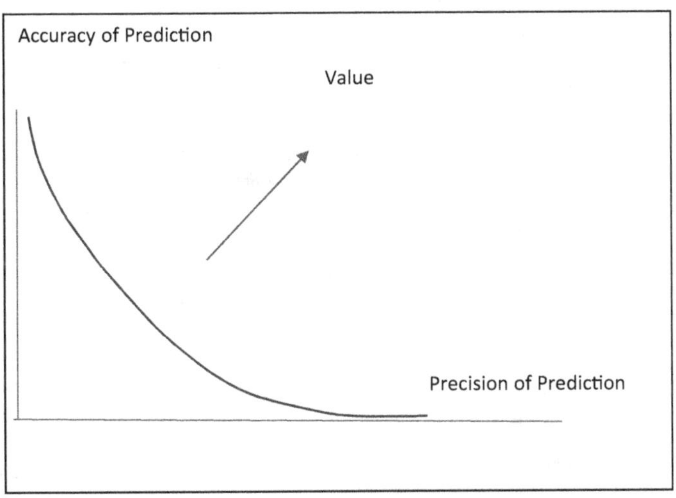

Figure 1.10. The Predictive Trade-Off

Since all prediction involves some human elements of observation and formulation, it follows that all prediction is also affected by Expectation Influenced Probability. This affects how we manage risks.

Of course, prediction is anyway a problem. See Figure 1.10.

Typically, there is a trade-off between the precision and accuracy of prediction. However, prediction is only meaningful and useful when it has high precision AND accuracy, and when it's well founded. It only works when we have realistic models, parameterising data, and other factors held constant.

But, it has been abused. Nostradamus and the Oracle of Delphi could be said to have achieved high predictive accuracy by vague, open, low accuracy predictions. But, in recent times, we have in particular seen an attempt to move to very precise prediction, with a consequence, of course, that we don't get much accuracy.

The belief that Prediction is Failing is widespread. Google gives over 44 million results although some are perhaps in the wrong context (See Figure 1.11.).

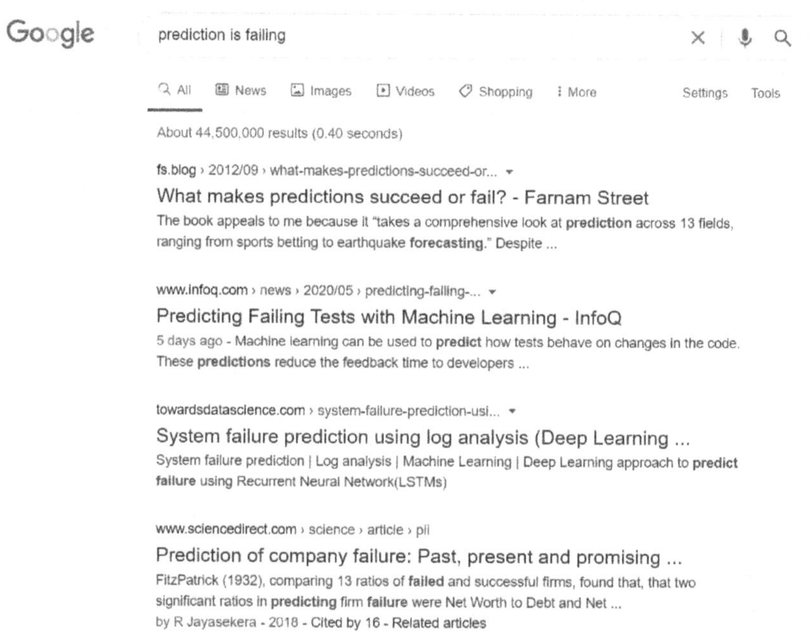

Google prediction is failing

All News Images Videos Shopping More Settings Tools

About 44,500,000 results (0.40 seconds)

fs.blog › 2012/09 › what-makes-predictions-succeed-or...

What makes predictions succeed or fail? - Farnam Street

The book appeals to me because it "takes a comprehensive look at **prediction** across 13 fields, ranging from sports betting to earthquake **forecasting**." Despite ...

www.infoq.com › news › 2020/05 › predicting-failing-...

Predicting Failing Tests with Machine Learning - InfoQ

5 days ago - Machine learning can be used to **predict** how tests behave on changes in the code. These **predictions** reduce the feedback time to developers ...

towardsdatascience.com › system-failure-prediction-usi...

System failure prediction using log analysis (Deep Learning ...

System failure prediction | Log analysis | Machine Learning | Deep Learning approach to **predict failure** using Recurrent Neural Network(LSTMs)

www.sciencedirect.com › science › article › pii

Prediction of company failure: Past, present and promising ...

FitzPatrick (1932), comparing 13 ratios of **failed** and successful firms, found that, that two significant ratios in **predicting** firm **failure** were Net Worth to Debt and Net ...

by R Jayasekera - 2018 - Cited by 16 - Related articles

Figure 1.11. Extract from Google for 'prediction is failing' in May 2020

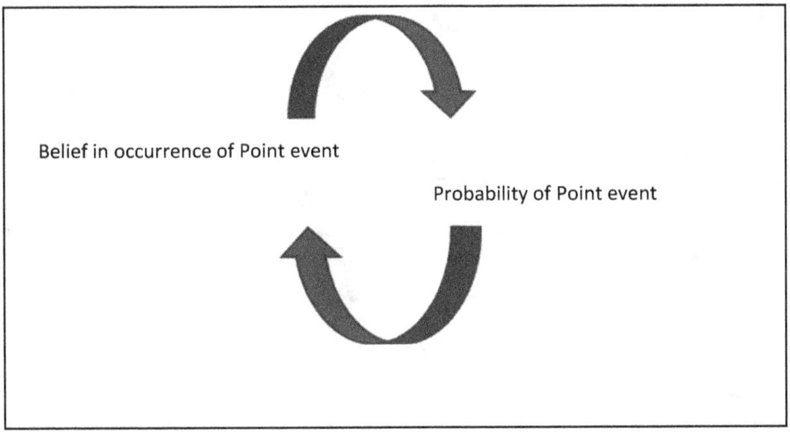

Figure 1.12. Expectation Influenced Probability
Source: The Anti-Fragility Academy.

So, whether we are considering Risk Analysis, Black Swans or market bubbles, it is easy to think that they, like perhaps so much else today, are unpredictable.

Over and above this, Expectation Influenced Probability comes into play in special circumstances when peoples' predictions, assessments or beliefs of what is going to happen directly or indirectly affect people's actions, which in turn affect what does happen.

Under Expectation Influenced Probability, the degree of belief affects the probability or frequency of occurrence, but in general this will then in turn affect the degree of belief, giving a closed causal loop. This could be either a Reinforcing or a Balancing Loop, dependent on the circumstances. See Figure 1.12.

For example, in Risk Management, we deliberately work to mitigate or reduce the probabilities of occurrence of undesirable major hazards so that a Balancing Loop is created as in Figure 1.13.

In contrast, for a market bubble, without other intervention, a Reinforcing Loop arises, as in Figure 1.14, because of the 'Bandwagon effect'. A given expected growth in value then attracts in funds which then increase price and value.

In general, under Expectation Influenced Probability, Balancing or Reinforcing Loops can arise.

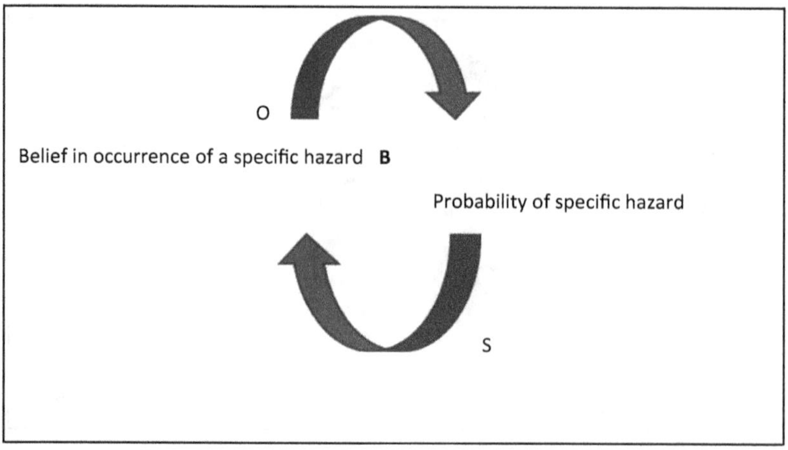

Figure 1.13. Application of Expectation Influenced Probability to Risk Management
Source: The Anti-Fragility Academy.

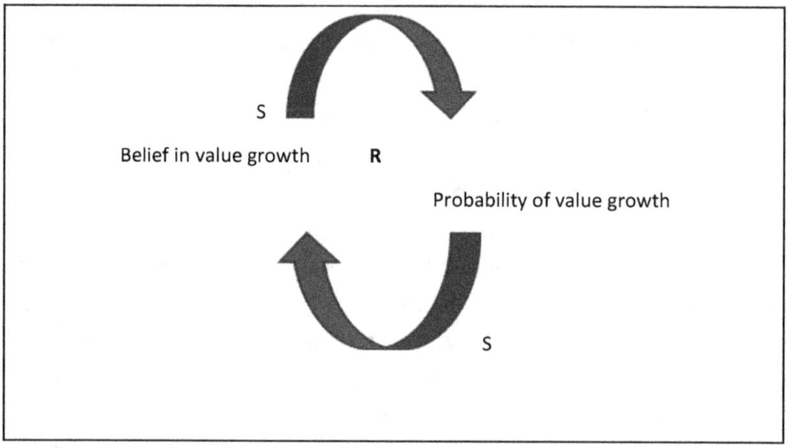

Figure 1.14. Application of Expectation Influenced Probability to a Market Bubble
Source: The Anti-Fragility Academy.

In Expectation Influenced Probability, Black Swans may represent circumstances in which we start with no awareness of the possibility of something occurring, expectation zero, but then possibly triggered by a point event, our belief in the possibility of it increases to such an extent

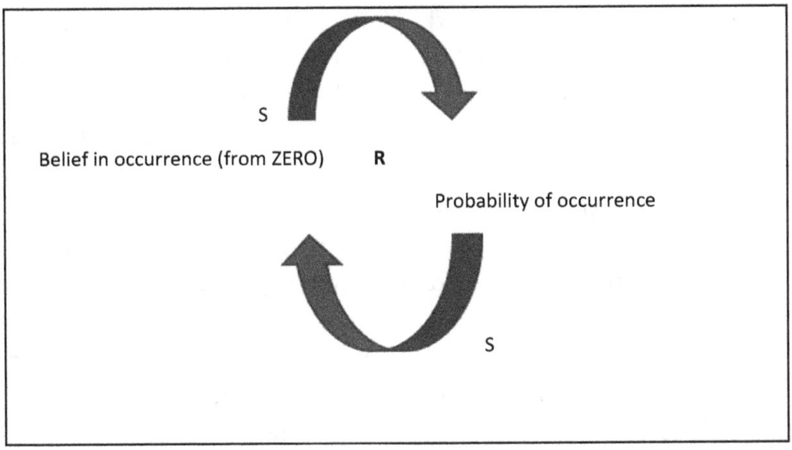

Figure 1.15. Application of Expectation Influenced Probability to a Black Swan
Source: The Anti-Fragility Academy.

that it becomes possible or likely to occur, pushing up the probability in a Reinforcing Loop. (See Figure 1.15.) An example may be a run on the banks or a Financial Crisis, triggered by a news story or rumour.

So, considering Global Crises, we can also see their propagation similarly as to Reinforcing Loops in which the population's expectation drives up the probability of the Crisis outcome.

Return from the Black Hole: Entrepreneurship, a Sense of Time, Resilience and Emergence

However, unless the worst possible outcome of all sorts is to occur, at some point in the propagation of the Crisis, there is a discernible transition into the resolution phase. The mechanism for this switch may be varied and complex. At the simplest level, logistic growth may reflect a self-limiting Crisis, as the susceptible population becomes saturated so that there are insufficient numbers still at risk to maintain its growth rate.

In terms of Soft Systems Thinking, we can think of this switch as the emergence of the dominance of a Balancing Loop, over and above the original Reinforcing Loop propagating the Crisis.

In returning from the 'Black Hole' of the Crisis, or equivalently switching into the resolution phase, the key factors are Entrepreneurship, a Sense of Time, Resilience and Emergence. These reflect the importance of divergent and lateral thinking amongst the population or key players, such as the government, to break the power of the ongoing cycle, Reinforcing Loop or Vicious Circle.

Each of the four reflects a slightly different mechanism. As a vicious circle propagates the Crisis, Entrepreneurship provides the opportunity for participants in the population to identify and seize opportunities made possible by the Crisis itself. For example, if as a result of the Crisis interest rates or prices drop substantially, this may provide the opportunity for new investment and entrepreneurship, providing new balance.

Governments will often act deliberately to mitigate Crises by encouraging such entrepreneurship through fiscal or other means. Furthermore, they themselves will often act entrepreneurially by intervening in a market or acting to seed changed behaviour.

Entrepreneurship may be political, societal or economic and is very linked to a Sense of Time, a belief that the time is now right for such an intervention and that the Crisis has reached a point where there is now an opportunity to, at minimum, resolve it or, at maximum, greatly profit from it.

How is such a sense of time created or determined? Does it emerge rather than be created? Do the most entrepreneurial sense it first, and the most risk-adverse last? Is it an emergent process in our heads, or is it triggered? Probably, some of all that.

Resilience is a factor that has kept the spirit and belief in the possibility of resolution and profit alive through the Crisis and protects our psychological and tangible assets ready for eventual re-emergence when the time is right.

Emergence itself is a process since the entrepreneurial steps need to be played out at the right times in the right sequence to challenge the power of the dominant Reinforcing Loop or Vicious Circle, based on the sense of time. Of course, they never quite are, but may still vanquish it.

We thus emerge from the Crisis.

The consequential requirements for Enterprise Risk Management: developing a sensible and reliable useful model

Enterprise Risk Management (ERM) is the best approach to managing risk we have, but there are many things wrong with the practice of Enterprise Risk Management today, particularly when we think in terms of Global Crises.

As we discussed in the Preface, ERM has many shortcomings, such as not including Black Swans or risks you cannot conceive, being difficult to implement, and in practice having limited effectiveness. In the context of Global Crises, ERM typically does not give adequate attention to the difference in nature of systemic risks and the need to treat them differently from local risks.

So, what are the consequential requirements for ERM given the overall model of Global Crises that we have developed in this chapter?

In Chapter 8, we discuss the continuing flow of global trends and Black Swans further, and also the objectives and infrastructure requirements to implement a more sensible Enterprise Risk Management system.

Here, as a start, we propose that there are six fundamental reinterpretations of the current ERM Model that are needed to adequately ensure a sensible reliable useful model. These are as follows:

1. *Mind the systemic gaps*: Risk and Continuity management in many organisations tends in practice to be local or 'bitty', often associated with continuing independent business streams or services. As an example, in the recent COVID-19 Crisis, a local government organisation with which I am connected found itself to have some 95 distinct unconnected untested Business Continuity plans (one for each service area), poor centralised coordination of human resources to address the crisis, poor centralised logistics for sourcing and distributing PPE across the authority, poor organisation-wide information flow and poor centralised coordinated decision-making. Such systemic gaps typically exist in the meta systems above operations and cause major

issues in organisational delivery in a Crisis. Within an organisation, **ERM needs to proactively address all such potential systemic gaps.**

2. *Not all risks are the same; Systemic Risks need to be treated differently*: The treatment of systemic risks in the same format as local risks, such as flooding, was discussed in the Preface. As we said there, in this way, Risk Management can fail to take account of the way Global Crises initiate, propagate and dissipate and so becomes inefficient and ineffective. Within the organisation, **ERM must differentiate the planning and control activities within the three phases of a crisis,** not treat the Crisis as an instantaneous risk with instantaneous impact. At all levels, **risks need to be managed through the three phases** and ignoring the phases negates the management of the risk of Crisis, instead treating it as purely an aggregated chance of disaster with an aggregated response to mitigate or manage its effects. So, **the structure of Risk Registers should change.**
3. *Join up Risk and Continuity*: With multiple ISO and other international standards, and often separated roles and responsibilities, it is not unusual for there to be a disconnect between Business Continuity Management, often seen as local, and Risk Management, seen as global and higher levels. This can mean that Risk Management does not adequately address the threats to Business Continuity that may be experienced. The above local government example is a good illustration of this in relation to the lack of treatment of systemic risks to Business Continuity in a crisis associated with logistics, human resources and information. So, **within the organisation, ERM should always take a unified holistic view of Business Continuity and Risk.**
4. *Mobilise early*: Also discussed in the Preface was the fact that it is not common organisational practice today for an organisation to proactively monitor and manage its response to an emerging Crisis, with many organisations only becoming somewhat proactive when sometime after initiation the Crisis enters the propagation or contagion phase. At this point, industry guidance, regulator requirements or government entreaty may precipitate organisational action, unfortunately, possibly somewhat late, even in high-risk situations. As an illustration, consider the COVID-19 Crisis. Despite

- clear warning of the next global pandemic going back at least a decade,
- early warning of the emerging threat within China at the beginning of the year,
- explicit evidence of the pandemic starting to spread internationally,
- clear emergence into a global phenomenon, and subsequently,
- development into a severe local threat,

little organisational attention was given to it, or responsive actions instigated, by many organisations until instructed or asked to do so by the central government authority as 'the fat hit the pan' at the last of the above phases. **ERM within the organisations needs greater awareness, monitoring and proactivity with active business continuity and risk management and mitigation throughout all these phases**.

5. *Protect yourself from what you cannot conceive*: Despite Precautionary Principles being established in Environmental Management, they are not yet a major part of ERM. Unfortunately, this can mean that if only specific risks are included in the Risk Register, then unknown and unknowable risks, such as Black Swans, are in no way protected against. However, typically sensible safeguards can still protect us, in the same way that washing your hands will protect you from many, not specific, sources of infection. **The identification, establishment and constant application of appropriate Precautionary Principles should be an explicit part of ERM within an organisation**.
6. *Become Anti-Fragile*: Writing in April 2020 in an invited commentary about the current Global Crisis, former Governor of the Bank of England, Mark Carney, said in *The Economist* that

   We are entering a world in which firms will be expected to prepare for black swans by valuing anti-fragility ... and planning for catastrophe.

   Anti-fragility is a property, more than just resilience or robustness, whereby something actually gets stronger from being stressed. This can be achieved by **learning from and responding to stresses experienced and is a desirable property for any organisation pursuing ERM**.

2

Knowing the Crisis is Coming

Introduction

Chapter 2 concerns the shift in paradigms and mindset consequential on moving from the current unidimensional models of Crises and static formulations to a multidimensional and dynamic phased one. With the change in the nature of the concept of risk comes an associated need for a change in the meaning of Risk Management and, very specifically, the necessary roles of the Risk Manager and the Chief Risk Officer. The practice of Business Continuity and the role of the Business Continuity Manager also need to expand.

The recognition of the risk of Crisis and its more complex nature should also predicate associated fundamental changes in management practices throughout the organisation and across every phase of the Crisis. This chapter focuses on background awareness and preparedness, and upfront awareness and preparedness before a Crisis initiates, and the corresponding instigation and management of avoidance and mitigation.

Understanding and Responding to the Mechanisms Underlying Crises

As discussed in the Preface, there is going to be another Crisis, there are going to be many, and this background awareness, together with the associated understanding of its mechanisms as discussed in Chapter 1, should inform the management activities and practices of our organisations, and, indeed, our national governments and the global community. But today, in general terms, it doesn't.

Rather than talking here about Black, White and Grey Swans, there is an alternative formulation of initiating events for some Crises, like the COVID-19 Crisis, as Grey Rhinos. These are seen as highly probable, high impact but neglected threats. The terminology is associated with Michele Wucker, a policy analyst who publicised it in her 2016 book *The Grey Rhino: How to Recognize and Act on the Obvious Dangers We Ignore.* Grey Rhinos are, therefore, akin to both White and Grey Swans but also to 'the Elephant in the Room'.

Let's consider the COVID-19 Crisis. The World Health Organisation and other experts have for years been warning that a global pandemic can and, indeed, will happen. During previous outbreaks, such as Ebola and SARS, Europe was spared. This time it is not the case.

In writing about the COVID-19 Crisis, Wucker wrote the following:

> *Given what we know about pandemics and their increasing likelihood, outbreaks are highly probable and high impact. I coined the term "grey rhino" for exactly such events: obvious, visible, coming right at you, with large potential impact and highly probable consequences.*

The point here is that organisational management, national government, the global community and ALL OF US, consistently ignore highly obvious upcoming threats. Indeed, Grey Rhinos are not random surprises but typically occur after a series of warnings and visible evidence. Examples are the bursting of the housing bubble in 2008, the devastating aftermath of Hurricane Katrina and other natural disasters, the new digital technologies that upended the media world, and the fall of the Soviet Union; all of these were evident to the observant and aware well in advance. But it could be said that little was done as a result.

Highly obvious, but ignored, threats can do, and do do, enormous damage. Understanding the mechanisms underlying Crises is part of the issue but acting on them accordingly is the other part. So, our issue here is actually about mindsets and behaviours. Agency theory causes us to question whether an organisation's people will always act in its best interests in regard to the risks of a Crisis.

Organisational culture, mindsets and behaviours affect how organisations and their people respond to risks and face up to, or not, a looming Crisis. The current organisational culture of Risk Management in many organisations sees it as a necessary safeguard, partially at least a compliance issue, and as a separate superimposed function on the back of Operations, not fully strategic and an added cost.

ERM can be seen as so high level, about the total enterprise position, that looming crises are not its main 'bread and butter' and are largely seen as business continuity issues.

In terms of Business Continuity Management, this is seen essentially as Incident Management or Emergency Management at best, separated from and more operational than Risk Management, and largely about short term continuity. Generally, no one is eager to declare an emergency, and within organisations, we tend to wait until it is demonstratively necessary.

It is also well established in Risk Management that people are not good at estimating risk and vary in their response to it. They can both overestimate and underestimate risk, or both at once, as when they buy both car insurance and a lottery ticket, that is, at the same time overestimating the probability that one rare event will occur, while underestimating another, be it the theft of a car or picking the winning numbers.

Psychological economics studies identify two opposing responses that characterise people facing an opportunity or a risk which has a low probability of occurring.

The most familiar response is increased sensitivity to a risk. For example, in the case of the coronavirus pandemic, this response triggers behaviour motivated by panic, like emptying supermarket shelves, or a national leadership's overreaction to that panic and the implementation of severe measures that will do excessive damage to the economy.

The second reaction, underestimation of risk is thought to be rarer. In the case of the pandemic, this tendency can lead to indifference to the risk, which affects behaviours, such as not social distancing, and leads to a more rapid spread of the virus as a result. This, in turn, leads to a rapid rise in the number of people infected and the collapse of the health system.

Recent work in Israel during the COVID-19 Crisis suggests that the deviation toward overestimation of the risk is stronger only when people react to a description of the problem in advance, while when people are experiencing the circumstances directly linked to the problem itself, they tend to underestimate the risk. Then, most decision makers operate in accordance with the view that 'it won't happen to me/us.'"

So, based on this argument, how organisations and their people respond to a looming Crisis and face up to it, or not, in taking action could suffer early on if employees overestimate the risks, and is likely to deteriorate as the Crisis becomes more imminent as underestimation of the risk of the Crisis itself may become more prevalent.

Risk Management, the Risk Manager and the Chief Risk Officer

As we said above, understanding the mechanisms underlying Global Crises and moving from the current unidimensional models of crises and static formulations to a multidimensional and dynamic phased one imply a consequential shift in paradigms and mindset. With the change in the nature of the concept of risk comes an associated need for a change in the meaning of Risk Management and, very specifically, the necessary roles of the Risk Manager and the Chief Risk Officer.

As a start, let us remember that, ignoring the special phased nature of Crises, typically *Risk* is defined simply as the effect uncertainty has on the achievement of the organisation's objectives. ISO 31000: 2018 is based on defining Risk Management to then be the coordinated activities to direct and control an organisation with regard to risk. There is no direct reference to immediacy, nor time at all, in these definitions.

It is not surprising, therefore, to commonly find descriptions of the role of the Risk Manager, such as one below, or those in Figures 2.1 and 2.2.

> *The role of a Risk Manager is to communicate risk policies and processes for an organisation. They provide hands-on development of risk models involving market, credit and operational risk, assure controls are operating effectively, and provide research and analytical support.*

Risk Management job description guide| Robert Half January 2022.[1]

While the role description in Figure 2.2 perhaps goes a little further than the above quote and that in Figure 2.1, in emphasising the need

---

[1] https://www.roberthalf.com.au/employers/financial-services/risk-management-jobs.

Risk Manager responsibilities include:

- Identifying and analyzing various risks (e.g. business, financial)
- Developing risk management controls and contingency plans
- Communicating recommendations to management

Job brief

We are looking for a Risk Manager to advise us on various types of risks (business, financial, legal and security.) You will identify potential threats and create plans to prevent and mitigate problems.

In this role, you should be highly perceptive and methodical. You should also have the ability to communicate effectively and present your plans in a convincing way. If you have experience in risk assessment and financial analysis, we'd like to meet you.

Ultimately, you will ensure that our company secures its reputation and profitability by controlling risk.

Responsibilities

- Conduct assessments to define and analyze possible risks
- Evaluate the gravity of each risk by considering its consequences
- Audit processes and procedures
- Develop risk management controls and systems
- Design processes to eliminate or mitigate potential risks
- Create contingency plans to manage crises
- Evaluate existing policies and procedures to find weaknesses
- Prepare reports and present recommendations
- Help implement solutions and plans
- Evaluate employees' risk awareness and train them when necessary

Requirements

- Proven experience as a Risk Manager
- Knowledge of risk assessment and control
- Experience with auditing and reporting procedures
- Familiarity with industry compliance standards and regulations (e.g. Occupational Safety and Health Act)
- Strong computer and research skills; knowledge of analysis software is preferred (e.g. Statistical Analysis Software, or SAS)
- Analytical mind with problem-solving aptitude
- Excellent communication and presentation skills
- BSc/BA in Law, Business, Finance or a related field
- Professional Risk Manager (PRM) certification is a plus

AVAILABLE IN

English

Related Job Descriptions

Actuary job description
Compliance Manager job descriptior
Financial Analyst job description

Related Interview Questions

Risk Analyst interview questions
Compliance Manager interview questions
Finance Analyst interview questions

Related Topics

Six job posting guidelines to follow f job board approval
Top free job posting sites for employ
Best job boards: The ultimate job sit list

Figure 2.1. Risk Manager Job Description in May 2020

Source: https://resources.workable.com/risk-manager-job-description.

Job Descriptions > Industries > Risk Manager

Risk Manager Job Description: Skills, Duties, Requirements and Career

View all Risk Manager jobs on Jobted UK

Risk Manager Job Description

A **risk manager** is a person responsible for **analyzing, assessing and managing the risks** faced by an **enterprise**.

The job of a risk manager is to identify, anticipate and prevent all of the critical **financial, operational and safety** risks that may potentially harm the enterprise and develop strategies, processes and systems for monitoring and managing those risks and ensuring **business continuity**.

But what does a Risk Manager do, exactly?

A risk manager's first task is to carry out **investigations** and analyses and **gather data** in order to identify the internal and external risks to which the enterprise is exposed and on that basis define the enterprise's operational and financial **risk profile**. As part of this process, the risk manager analyses the enterprise's **key risk indicators (KRI)** and conducts '**what-if analyses**' to determine what the consequences would be if the risks identified were to actually occur. Potential consequences may include a financial loss, a loss of earnings, a breach of confidential information or damage to the enterprise's assets (e.g. products or infrastructure).

Based on the **risk analysis**, the risk manager performs an assessment of the company's risk management policies and procedures to determine whether the company has adequate controls in place in all areas of its operations. If this 'vulnerability assessment' reveals critical areas or weaknesses, the risk manager may propose changes or improvements to the organization's **risk policy** or **enterprise risk management system**.

Risk managers are also responsible for implementing **control systems** and **strategic action plans** designed to **protect the company's assets and resources** by preventing risks from occurring, mitigating the potential damage or transferring the risk to other parties.

The measures identified by a risk manager will naturally vary from organization to organization. For example, they may include formulating **business continuity plans** to respond to potential disruptions, defining **crisis management** processes, introducing new **operating protocols** or regulations, updating procedures in line with the latest standards and best practices, or taking out **insurance coverage**.

Some risks, however, are inherent in a company's operations – such as the risks associated with **financial market** transactions – and thus cannot be totally avoided. In these cases, risk managers are tasked with setting the level of risk that the company is prepared to accept (known as an organization's **risk appetite**) and developing strategies to keep its risk exposure below a certain threshold. A key role in this process is played by **documentation**. In order to support their assessments of the risks to which the company is exposed and enable the creation of the reports they periodically submit to the organization's management team, risk managers need **data** (e.g. **statistics**, business sector reports etc).

Risk managers use the information they gather to providing **advice and recommendations** to senior management on a range of risk management-related issues, for example proposing strengthening the IT infrastructure to enhance **cyber security**, automating a company's internal processes or adapting the business model to respond to emerging risks.

Risk managers are also responsible for proactively monitoring and identifying developments of a financial, social or legislative nature that may **impact on an organization's operational and strategic risk profile**.

In some cases, they may also have direct responsibility for the **implementation of the risk management plans** they propose and act in a quasi-project manager role, with a set budget and a delivery deadline. This typically involves working with managers and staff at all levels of the company to ensure that new procedures are followed and conducting **training** to educate personnel on the new risk policy and increase awareness of the risks associated with the organization's activities.

Another key element of the risk management process is carrying out **checks, stress tests and audits** (as part of a cycle of continuous review and improvement) to verify that the procedures and controls in place are effective and compliant with all the relevant **regulatory requirements**.

Risk managers are employed by public organizations and private companies in a wide range of sectors and industries. However, the majority of **vacancies for risk managers** can be found in banks and **financial services** companies, **insurance companies**, **construction** and **engineering** firms, **IT** and **telecommunications** companies, **auditing** firms and **consulting** groups specializing in **risk management**, and in the **healthcare** sector.

The work of a risk manager is largely **office-based**, although sometimes business trips may be necessary in order to assess risks associated with specific operations or workplaces, present risk analyses and assessments to management or investors, or to provide clients with risk consultancy services.

Figure 2.2. Risk Manager Job Description May 2020
Source: (https://uk.jobted.com/job-description/risk-manager)

A **risk manager**'s primary **tasks** and **responsibilities** include:

- Analysing company risk profile
- Presenting risk assessment to senior management team and company directors
- Devising effective risk management strategies
- Monitoring key risk indicators
- Regularly reviewing internal risk policy and ensuring compliance with new legislation
- Actively contributing to implementation of risk management plan and involving all personnel in process
- Training personnel on risk management principles and raising awareness of risk within organization
- Designing monitoring systems to maintain level of risk below established threshold
- Writing periodic reports for management and providing advice and recommendations on risk management related issues

How to Become a Risk Manager - Education, Training and Requirements

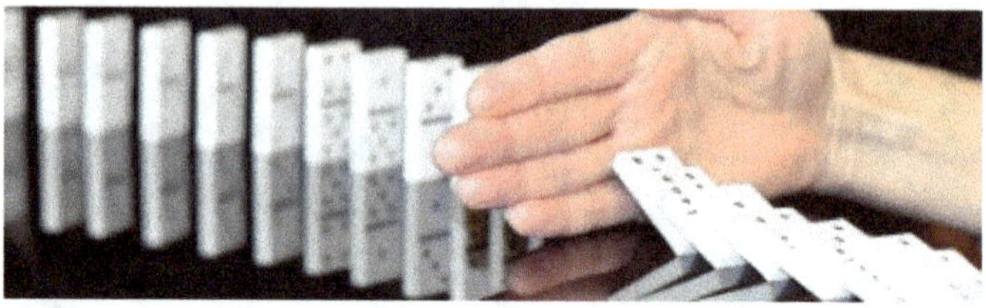

To **become a risk manager** typically requires a degree in **statistics, economics, business and finance, mathematics, IT** or in another **scientific field.** In addition to knowledge in a range of cross-cutting areas, such as data analytics, corporate governance, risk management, internal audit, regulatory compliance, security, quality assurance, and an understanding of **risk assessment models**, the job also calls **significant prior experience in a risk management role** - for example in an insurance or financial setting or with an auditing or consulting firm.

For positions managing risks in very specific areas, such as IT or engineering, candidates may be required to have specialist qualifications and technical knowledge, including of the relevant **regulatory framework** and the **national and international standards and best practices for risk management**. Finally, candidates holding specific **risk management qualifications** are likely to be preferred.

Risk Manager Skills and Qualifications

The key **skills** and qualities required by a **risk manager** include:

- Knowledge of risk assessment models
- Knowledge of auditing and reporting procedures
- Knowledge of actuarial and statistical tools
- Ability to implement risk monitoring and testing procedures
- Ability to use office automation tools
- Excellent verbal and written communication skills
- Ability to build relationships with key stakeholders
- Analytical skills
- Attention to detail
- Organizational and time management skills
- Team player but ability to work independently
- Proactivity

Figure 2.2. (*Continued*)

for operational responsiveness and activity, all descriptions are focused primarily on an analysing, awareness and planning role, and do not define the role fundamentally as an operational one focused on real-time, live managing of evolving risks.

Perhaps we could argue that in the past, before the current turbulent times, the many Swans and the odd Grey Rhinoceros, that was not necessary for the role, or at least it was less obviously needed when the Swans and Rhinoceroses were less apparent. Perhaps.

Also, perhaps, the convenient notional separation of Risk Management from Business Continuity Management enabled Risk Management to be seen largely as an analytical and planning activity, while Business Continuity Management involved real operational response to a Crisis.

However, this presupposes a real phase disconnect between the analysing, awareness and planning of Risk Management, and the subsequent operational responsiveness of Business Continuity Management. Given the nature of Global Crises, with their three phases of instigation, propagation and resolution, such a disconnect makes no sense from a management perspective, since we are arguing strongly that operational responsiveness is needed earlier in the instigation and propagation phases.

With the development of Enterprise Risk Management, the role of Chief Risk Officer has also emerged. Does this perhaps close the operational shortfall in the role coverage of the Risk Manager? Unfortunately, largely not.

If we look at role descriptions for Chief Risk Officers, we see that, according to Wikipedia,[2]

> *The chief risk officer (CRO) or chief risk management officer (CRMO) of a firm or corporation is the executive accountable for enabling the efficient and effective governance of significant risks, and related opportunities, to a business and its various segments. Risks are commonly categorised as strategic, reputational, operational, financial, or compliance-related. CROs are accountable to the Executive Committee and The Board for enabling the business to balance risk and reward. In more complex organisations, they are generally responsible for coordinating the organisation's Enterprise Risk Management (ERM) approach. The CRO is responsible for assessing*

[2] https://en.wikipedia.org/wiki/Chief_risk_officer (May 2020).

> *and mitigating significant competitive, regulatory, and technological threats to a firm's capital and earnings. The CRO's roles and responsibilities vary depending on the size of the organisation and industry. The CRO works to ensure that the firm is compliant with government regulations, such as Sarbanes–Oxley, and reviews factors that could negatively affect investments. Typically, the CRO is responsible for the firm's risk management operations, including managing, identifying, evaluating, reporting and overseeing the firm's risks externally and internally to the organisation and works diligently with senior management, such as the Chief Executive officer and Chief Financial Officer.*

On the Other hand, Investopedia defines a Chief Risk Officer as follows[3]:

> *A chief risk officer (CRO) is an executive in charge of managing risks to the company. It is a senior position that requires years of experience in accounting, economics, legal, or actuarial background. The role of the chief risk officer is constantly evolving, as technologies and business practices change.*

Other role descriptions reinforce this view, as we see in Figures 2.3 and 2.4 below.

The Business Continuity Manager and Their Relationship to Risk Management

What then of the Business Continuity Manager? While there is perhaps some confusion in a few places with the Risk Management role, e.g., https://resources.infosecinstitute.com/job-titles/business-continuity-manager/#gref, in general, Business Continuity Managers are seen as having an operational dimension.

The international standard for Business Continuity, 'ISO 22301: 2019 Security and Resilience — Business Continuity Management Systems — Requirements', uses a definition of Business Continuity as

> *capability of an organisation to continue the delivery of products and services within acceptable time frames at predefined capacity during a disruption.*

---

[3] https://www.investopedia.com/terms/c/chief-risk-officer-cro.asp (May 2020).

The Chief Risk Officer

The Chief Risk Officer (CRO) position is relatively new, but gaining traction. The CRO is responsible for planning, implementing, directing, and administering a company's enterprise risk management program to achieve maximum profitabili

The successful CRO typically has a college degree in business, economics, finance or engineering, and over 10 years experience in a broad range of business functionalities. This broad experience ensures the CRO is familiar with all business risks that are present within a company, including strategic, financial, operational, and hazard risks.

The CRO is a high level executive whose main responsibilities include:

1. Working closely with senior management to develop and carry-out a company's enterprise risk management program
2. Formally identifying and documenting specific risks in the strategic, operational, financial, and hazard risk centers
3. Understanding, assessing and quantifying underlying risk associated with a company's risk centers and reporting those risks for top level management
4. Identifying and communicating with senior and functional management about risks that may impact a company's profitabilit or cause a financial loss
5. Setting risk control priorities in response to the risk mitigation requests set forth by senior management
6. Coordinating and overseeing implementation of risk controls in various departments to reduce and transfer risk
7. Evaluating the success of risk controls and monitoring their status over time
8. Implementing and updating the framework, policies and processes under which risk assessment is performed and risk controls are placed, including determining action items, scheduling mitigation activities, and implementing schedules to ensure early detection, management and mitigation of risks
9. Analyzing historical risk exposure and loss trending to implement best practices throughout a company's corporate structure.

Figure 2.3. Chief Risk Officer Job Description in May 2020
Source: http://www.erm360.com/erm-process/the-chief-risk-officer/.

The big question is how much does the Business Continuity Manager's primary role, focused on maintaining operations through the Crisis, interrelate with the Risk Managers and Chief Risk Officers' roles, which as we have seen are focused more on analysing, awareness and planning.

While Business Continuity Managers do, typically, have some planning aspects to their roles, the answer is probably not enough. As we said in Chapter 1, with multiple ISO and other international standards, and often separated roles and responsibilities, it is not unusual for there to be a disconnect between Business Continuity Management, often seen as local, and Risk Management, seen as global and higher levels. This can mean that Risk Management does not adequately address the threats to Business Continuity that may be experienced.

Defining New Role Definitions

So, in order to deal more adequately with Global Crises, how should the roles of the Risk Manager, the Business Continuity Manager and the Chief Risk Officer change?

As we said at the end of Chapter 1, there is a need for a more unified holistic view of Business Continuity and Risk, within an Enterprise Risk Management framework. More specifically, Risk Management should be

Learn about the Chief Risk Officer role in Data Protection 101, our series on the fundamentals of information security.

The Chief Risk Officer is a C-suite executive who is tasked with the identification, analysis, and mitigation of events that could threaten a company. These risks could be internal or external in nature.

The CRO helps ensure that their organization is compliant with regulations set forth by the government, including the **Dodd-Frank Wall Street Reform and Consumer Protection Act of 2010** and the **Sarbanes-Oxley Act**. The CRO also reviews different factors that could adversely impact the company's investors or the performance of its business units.

Another name for the CRO is the Chief Risk Management Officer.

WHAT DOES A CHIEF RISK OFFICER DO?

A Chief Risk Officer is tasked with looking out for a variety of risks that can be categorized into three groups: technical, regulatory, and competitive. A CRO must also monitor procedures that might give rise to risk exposure. For instance, if a company collects data from their customers, suppliers, or other third parties, they will need to make sure that all that **data is safe and kept confidential**. If there is a security lapse, the CRO would need to address the issue to ensure that it does not happen again.

There are also physical risks involved. For instance, if a company sends employees to somewhat dangerous areas, then the CRO will need to create procedures and policies that will address these added threats. In a warehouse facility, the CRO will be tasked with ensuring that the staff is kept out of harm's way.

Because a company's operating environment is always changing, the CRO must always have a plan of action to proactively and reactively **manage these risks**. Sometimes, that can even mean modifying established policies and procedures on the fly in order to address vulnerabilities and risks.

CHIEF RISK OFFICER RESPONSIBILITIES

A CRO leads efforts to reduce business risks that can put an organization's profitability and productivity at risk. They also spearhead efforts related to enterprise risk management.

Figure 2.4. Chief Risk Officer: What is a CRO? (and Why You Need One) by Juliana De Grout on Tuesday, September 18, 2018
Source: https://digitalguardian.com/blog/chief-risk-officer-what-cro-and-why-you-need-one.

A Chief Risk Officer is responsible for implementing policies and procedures to minimize or manage operational risks. They are also tasked with coming up with mitigating processes to help minimize or avoid losses that may arise when the systems, procedures, or policies in place are found to be inadequate – or if they fail entirely.

A CRO must manage **compliance** with regulatory requirements on a federal, state, and local level. They are also concerned with other security-related issues, including IT security, internal auditing, financial auditing, insurance, fraud prevention, global business climate changes, and similar corporate internal investigations. They may also become involved with disaster recovery and business continuity planning.

As one would guess, the responsibilities of a Chief Risk Officer largely depend on an organization's size as well as its industry. The CRO is responsible for all risk management strategies and operations, as well as supervising the organization's risk mitigation and identification procedures.

In recent years, IT has become a big part of every business and naturally, the CRO needs to address the risks associated with data breaches and hackers. As such, the CRO is also concerned with **risk assurance and data protection** and has a hand in stamping out system vulnerabilities and other threats.

Aside from these, the responsibilities of a CRO include:

- Developing risk maps and formulating strategic action plans to help minimize, manage, and mitigate primary risks and then monitor the progress of these efforts.
- Creating and disseminating risk analysis reports and progress reports to different stakeholders, including employees, board members, and C-suite executives.
- Ensuring that risk management priorities are reflected in the company's strategic plans.
- Formulating and implementing risk assurance strategies that are related to the transmission, storage, and use of information and data systems.
- Evaluating possible operational risks that may arise from human error or system failures, which might disrupt or affect business processes. The CRO also develops different strategies to minimize risk exposure and designates appropriate responses for when human errors or system failures occur.
- Measuring the organization's risk appetite, and setting the amount of risk that the organization is able – and willing – to take on.
- Developing budgets for risk-related projects and supervising their funding
- Conducting risk assurance and due diligence on behalf of the organization in the events of mergers, acquisitions, and business deals.

Figure 2.4. (*Continued*)

interpreted as including both *the forward* planning and control of risk, and the neglected *real-time* planning and control as the hazard is realised, and the 'fat hits the pan'; the latter currently being seen often as *only* a Business Continuity issue not really a Risk Management one.

In the context of Global Crises, this new unified holistic view is crucial, since the three phases of instigation, propagation and resolution require not just planning but operational responsiveness in each and every phase, in a unified responsive managed flow. There is no room for an artificial separation into forward Risk Management and subsequently only Business Continuity Management.

This means that the three roles of the Risk Manager, the Business Continuity Manager and the Chief Risk Officer need to change so that the two with Risk in their titles are more proactive operationally, not just planning but responding to the hazards and controlling risk in operations in real time as the Crisis unfolds, and the Business Continuity Manager is not just dealing with managing operations through the Crisis but also together with the Risk Manager or Chief Risk Officer is planning and deploying the staged response to the phased Crisis.

This suggests an at least partial convergence of roles, but the importance of Business Continuity through a Crisis is such that a specific role of Business Continuity Manager would still be sensible since, in a sense, the Business Continuity Manager can focus on keeping operations going/recovering operations no matter what, while the Risk Manager can focus on minimising the risk to operations, i.e., not letting it go wrong in the first place. The two roles are distinct.

Changes in Management Practice: Being Aware and Being Prepared

Once we accept that there will be another Crisis, it is not a major stretch to expect all management practices across the organisation to be sensitised to continually being aware and being prepared for its occurrence, ahead of the identification of its initiation.

The people of our organisation are our organisational 'eyes and ears' and sensibly we should have these alert to future threats, without having to wait until it is announced.

How else should management practice change? The challenge is to work to change the culture and assumption of 'normal' being 'business as usual'. During the COVID-19 Crisis, the term 'the new normal' became commonplace but far from fully defined. It was partly used to define the continuation of the 'lockdown' and 'don't leave home unless you must' arrangements of that Crisis. But it was also used to refer to how our personal and professional lives will be permanently altered by the coronavirus pandemic.

At the time, an interesting article in Forbes[4] covered aspects about workers having the option to continue to work from home long term and the implications for communication and work tracking. These are important areas as potential changes in management practice but so is the need for continual awareness and preparation for Crisis.

At the end of Chapter 1, we reported that Mark Carney, former Governor of the Bank of England, said in an invited commentary about that Crisis in *The Economist* magazine:

> *We are entering a world in which firms will be expected to prepare for black swans by valuing anti-fragility ... and planning for catastrophe.*

So, it is reasonable to postulate that, to deal more effectively with Global Crises, we need to see management practice change towards a more Anti-Fragile model. I wrote about the need for this myself in my 2014 Gower book *Building Anti-Fragile Organisations: Risk, Opportunity and Governance in a Turbulent World.*

In broad terms, this implies changes in management practice in all parts and levels of the organisation and at all layers within Deloitte's Layer Model. Part of this is to reduce the high emphasis on efficiency, and even effectiveness, and to focus more on reducing fragility and enabling the organisations to get stronger over time, as they are subject to stress.

At the top level, organisational governance, strategic management and risk management need to change. In addition to changing the organisational culture, to increase Anti-Fragility people management, operational process management, information management, technology management, innovation management, and supply chain management also need attention.

An Anti-Fragile organisation will, in general, be highly aware of its broad environment, including all threats and opportunities, wherever they arise in the sustainability space. As part of their standard management practice, they will constantly scan their horizons and be prepared to act accordingly, dependent on what they see.

[4] https://www.forbes.com/sites/laurelfarrer/2020/05/12/the-new-normal-isnt-remote-work-its-better/#3fcf69fb2405 on May 12, 2020.

In the context of potential upcoming Global Crisis then, horizon scanning needs to include the identification and monitoring of the initiating and propagating Crises, with both resultant forward planned and immediate Risk Management and mitigation, on an evolving emergent basis.

Avoiding Static Formulations

'Business as usual' reflects a static world view, in which organisational leadership, management and staff are not sensitised to be aware of potential upcoming out of the ordinary challenges or changes. For organisations established within slow-changing markets, or in slow-moving times, business as usual can easily be the default norm. In such organisations, there is not just a lack of awareness of threats but also typically a resistance to change.

In such organisations, Risk Management is often a compliance-driven ritual. Serious new threats are not revealed unless they happen.

The challenge for such organisations in such turbulent times as the present is to become, and stay, alert and proactive. This can be done in a number of ways or with a number of alternative focuses.

Within organisations, Change programmes can be concerned with 'one-off' step-changes in organisational culture, structure, systems, processes and work methods in response to a 'burning platform', but frequently incorporate sensibly some element of openness to ongoing change, for example, through continuous improvement activities.

Other examples are Lean and Six Sigma programmes, where inbuilt into the philosophy of the approach and infrastructure are ongoing improvement imperatives.

The problem is that these types of improvement programmes can have a very narrow, mainly internal focus, being aware and open to the possibilities of internal process change, but effectively excluding external horizon scanning, awareness and proactive response. This issue is reinforced by organisational structures that frequently restrict such activities to Operations.

For these reasons, organisational Benchmarking can be very useful in helping to mobilise awareness and preparedness in response to developing threats. Unfortunately, even where done, and done properly, Benchmarking is often again restricted to specific process, product or service issues.

In summarising, **unfortunately, organisations that are not aware of external threats are typically not aware that they are not aware**. Of course, it could be said that these don't recognise that they need horizon scanning until it's too late to do them any good, to save them from the threat.

As we have implied above, today, probably all organisations, and all people, are guilty of this to some extent. We must all be more alert to unexpected possibilities and be prepared. There are many methods of horizon scanning, and these should be employed sensibly and appropriately.

Instigating and Managing Avoidance and Mitigation

At the organisational level, the instigation of avoidance and mitigation should rightly be first established prior to a specific threat on the horizon being visible. It is a precautionary move, creating essential organisational architecture and infrastructure, similar to the establishment of the organisational financial system.

Of course, typically, many Risk Management and Business Continuity Management systems are set up *a priori* in this way but may have limited scope in terms of only being focused on conceived hazards and treating these in an undifferentiated way, with systemic risks treated as point events, as if they were the same as local hazards.

Instead, the real need *a priori* is to establish a Crisis Management System that deeply embeds precautionary principles in business practice, keeps these under constant review, treats systemic risks in terms of the phased nature of their hazards, and focuses on horizon scanning and organisational information gathering and processing in real time in order to identify, and be able to respond in real time to, phased emergence and progression through a Crisis in terms of avoidance and mitigation.

Such a system is also likely to be highly customised to the specific organisation since justifiably the level of complexity is considerably greater than generic 'off the shelf' risk management systems.

Naturally, it takes a lot more thinking, analysis and discussion to establish and instigate such a Crisis Management system than for the standard 'off the shelf' Risk Management ones we see in the majority of organisations today. Managing it is also considerably more difficult since the necessary increased complexity and customisation to the organisation's specific context mean that constant observation and review of the system itself are also needed as this may/will change over time, with resultant adjustment.

In a sense, the National and Global levels clearly match the Organisational one; i.e., there is a need to develop and maintain a complex, highly customised Crisis Management model of the national or global system that is potentially under threat.

3

Seeing the Crisis is Coming

Introduction

Once a specific Crisis initiates, the faster it is identified, analysed and specifically responded to by organisations, the better. Naturally, it is to be hoped for, and worked for, that this will be before the full impact of the Crisis is clearly visible.

Could we have identified previous Crises earlier? The answer is, of course, typically yes. But we do need to balance the two opposite risks of not identifying and responding to a genuine Crisis early and responding in a disproportionate sense to something which is not really a Crisis but could have become one. The former means that we inadequately prepare for and mitigate the upcoming Crisis, typically having to 'play catch up' too late at a high cost. The latter disrupts activities, wastes resources and, if it happens too frequently, may prevent us from responding early enough to a real Crisis.

To do this balancing, we need very good information systems and very good decision rules, but we also need to be specifically 'on the ball' when a specific Crisis initiates and starts to propagate.

How can we see it's coming? In this chapter, we discuss the propagation timescales of Crises and their acceleration. We consider how to organise for real-time observation and monitoring of initiating sequences and events at the organisational level, and how to plan and control avoidance, delay and mitigation based on this.

Being Observant and Being Prepared

If an organisation has put in place well the type of customised Crisis Management System and arrangements that we discussed at the end of Chapter 2, that deeply embeds precautionary principles in business practice, keeps these under constant review, treats systemic risks in terms of the phased nature of their hazards, and focuses on horizon scanning and organisational information gathering and processing in real time, then it should be well placed to respond well to a Crisis early.

However, being observant still requires avoiding 'business as usual' thinking and managing distractions, since the changes that need to be observed may appear very, too, minor to represent the initiation of a Crisis.

Being observant also covers consideration of all spheres in the sustainability space, and all identified potential dimensions and metrics. Fundamentally, all of this is about the need for an organisational Culture Change and an organisational and individual Mindset Change. Furthermore, in relation to culture and mindset changes, we are not talking about being observant and prepared for a clear single one-off initiation of a Crisis, or each Crisis. Rather for an accumulation of evidence and some false starts.

Changes in the status of emerging Crises subject to exponential growth appear very minor at the beginning but then escalate extremely rapidly to Crisis Point. If we don't spot the issue early on, it is already too late as the Crisis has grown to such an extent that we are needing major 'catch up'. As an example, consider the early history of COVID-19 cases recorded in the UK as depicted in Figure 3.1.

At what point would the epidemic become obvious? If we did not understand the propagating mechanism, then it's still pretty insignificant in terms of the total number of cases for the first half of March, so we would waste time rather than taking decisive actions. If we do understand the mechanism, we can see the rapid exponential growth and realise that we must be ready for thousands of cases by the end of the month.

We have discussed about being observant but what about preparedness? Once the organisation has put in place the customised Crisis Management System and arrangements discussed above, then if it remains observant, it essentially has the basis to respond well to a Crisis provided that it is prepared, and continuous observation or monitoring is followed by a

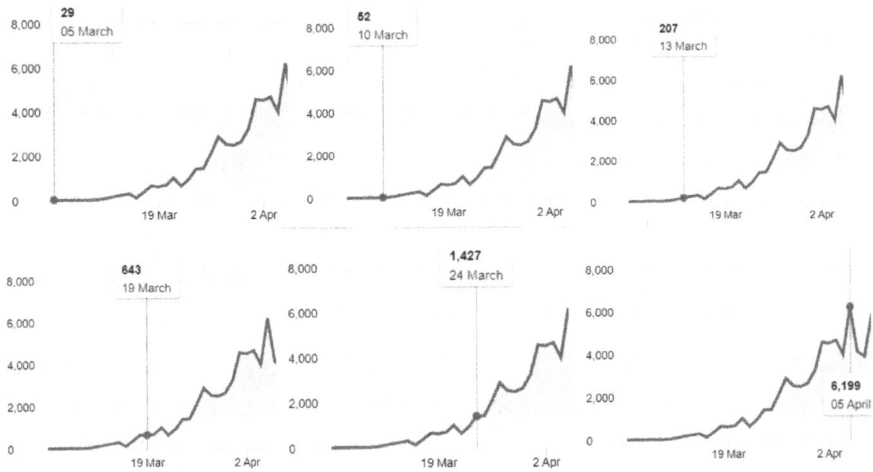

Figure 3.1. Early History of COVID-19 Cases Recorded in the UK in 2020

constant review. But, being really prepared, like being observant, can also be a challenge. This is about ensuring that the customised Crisis Management System and arrangements are fully maintained and operational to respond, in real time, to the looming threat, not once but on a continual basis as it unfolds.

The organisation can then determine the State of Threat, as well as manage its own State of Readiness. This emphasis on the state of threat and the state of readiness strongly suggests the need for an explicit organisational Crisis Management System that has the capabilities to mobilise its Crisis arrangements at an early stage.

Crisis Management Systems

The international Crisis Management standard Technical Specification PD CEN/TS 17091:2018 *Crisis management — Guidance for developing a strategic capability* is a reasonable first introduction to Crisis Management that broadly defines a Crisis as

> *an inherently abnormal, unstable and complex situation that represents a threat to the strategic objectives, reputation and, ultimately', the existence of an organisation.*

Table 1 in the Technical Specification provides a clear distinction between Incidents and Crises. Attempting to manage an extremely disruptive event as an incident rather than a Crisis can cause a delay before the Crisis is given meaningful strategic attention. The Technical Specification also provides a second definition of a Crisis as an

> *unprecedented or extraordinary event or situation that threatens an organisation and requires a strategic, adaptive, and timely response in order to preserve its viability and integrity.*

This Technical Specification also makes the point that the ability to manage crises cannot be simply deferred from consideration until the organisation is hit by a Crisis, global or otherwise. The arrangements that organisations have in place for managing routine disruptions are generally inadequate for Crises since these can be dynamic, unpredictable, and difficult to manage. Typically, a timely response to a Crisis is critical. Crises challenge organisations and their people, functions and processes and require a dynamic and dedicated management and response. In order to ensure the most effective transition to Crisis management status, the appropriate mobilisation of Crisis arrangements should be initiated as soon as we can ascertain that a Crisis is coming.

However, denial, complacency or delay in effective decision-making get in the way. Crises can be extraordinarily demanding and challenge staff perseverance, abilities, and competence. Flexibility and agility are needed. In addition, in Global Crises, in particular, staff and other stakeholders may be distraught, uncomfortable, outside their comfort zones or even traumatised.

So, real organisational Leadership is a key ingredient in any Crisis Management. This should be in evidence throughout the Crisis, as sustained effort is likely to be required. In particular, as soon as we see the Crisis is coming, there is a need for a clear decisive and immediate organisational call to action. To date in Global Crises, this has typically been missing.

An organisation needs a Crisis Management System, preferably documented, as the basis for managing, that's planning for and responding to, Crises. The basis for one is depicted in Figure 3.1 of PD CEN/TS 17091:2018, and this is reproduced in Figure 3.2.

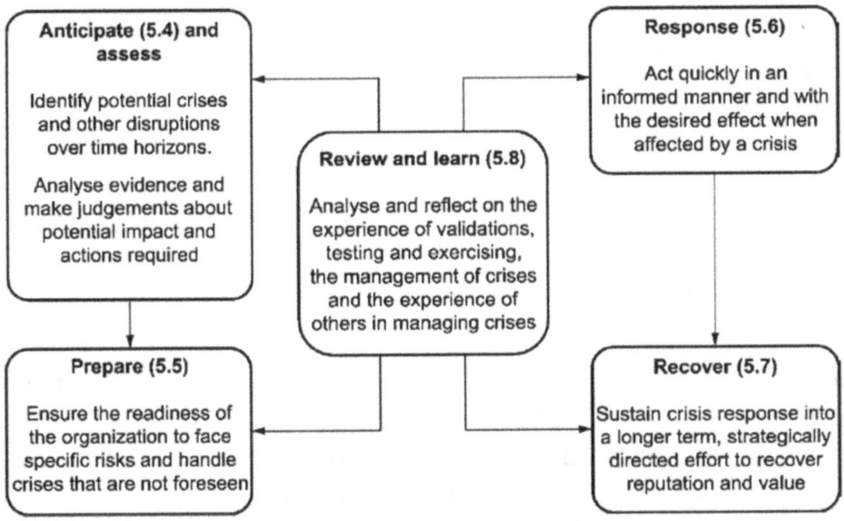

Figure 3.2. A Framework for Crisis Management

Source: Figure 3.1 of PD CEN/TS 17091:2018

Initiating Crisis Response at First Sighting

Unfortunately, PD CEN/TS 17091:2018 does not explicitly treat a Crisis as potentially phased and systemic, as we discussed in the Preface, but instead implicitly treats Crises as point events. The second definition of a Crisis given above explicitly refers to a Crisis as an event. The importance of this is clearer when seen in the context of the definition as it appears in the standard. See Figure 3.3.

The treatment of Crises as point events is illustrated both by the definition of a Crisis in Figure 3.3 and by the framework for Crisis Management contained in Figure 1 of the standard and reproduced above as Figure 3.2.

As the figure makes clear, the standard Response to the Crisis is seen as a unified imperative, taking place at a point in time or perhaps over a cognate period. In contrast to this approach contained in the PD CEN/TS 17091:2018 standard, we have argued in previous chapters that a Global Crisis is phased and systemic and that we must differentiate the planning and control activities within these phases. Thus, in terms of Response to

3.1
crisis
unprecedented or extraordinary event or situation that threatens an organization and requires a strategic, adaptive, and timely response in order to preserve its viability and integrity

Note 1 to entry: The event might include a high degree of uncertainty.

Note 2 to entry: The event might exceed the response capacity or capability of the organization.

Note 3 to entry: There is no adequate or appropriate plan to deal with the event such that a flexible and dynamic approach is needed.

Figure 3.3. The PD CEN/TS 17091:2018 Definition of 'Crisis'

the Crisis, we need to consider separately the responses to at minimum the phases within Crisis Initiation and Crisis Propagation. Here then, in Chapter 3, we consider the Response to Seeing that the Crisis is Coming.

The response to Seeing the Crisis is Coming should, as at all other stages or phases in Crisis Management, follow certain key principles. Clause 4.5 of the guidance in PD CEN/TS 17091:2018 stipulates that the overall response should be based on the following:

- trying to understand what is going on rather than just reacting to it
- achieving control as quickly as possible
- communicating effectively internally and externally
- ensuring clear transparent roles and responsibilities and structures
- building situational awareness through good information management and coordinated working
- having clear well-rehearsed decision-making and an initiation of action process in line with corporate values and objectives
- ensuring appropriate leadership and competence at all levels and areas
- ensuring policies, assumptions and decisions are appropriately documented, and
- learning from experience.

The response to Seeing the Crisis is Coming should be timely, fast and appropriately informed and have the desired effect since this is the first inhiation point for an emergency response. However, uncertainty is one of the defining aspects of Crises, so finding out what exactly is happening and understanding its implications are of high importance prior to action.

It is necessary nonetheless to accept that this required information may perforce be incomplete when decisions need to be taken and acted upon. Appropriate preplanning and training for evaluation and decision-making are, therefore, essential.

Crisis Response at First Sighting is likely to include a number of predefined key actions. These typically will encompass the following:

- verification of sighted Crisis potential and assessment of urgency,
- notification and mobilisation of key players, including executive management,
- initial Crisis business continuity planning and containment,
- review and reassessment of emergent risks,
- consideration of alternative Crisis propagation scenarios, strategies and prioritisation,
- initiation of Crisis Response Management, monitoring and coordination arrangements.

Identifying the State of Threat

The sighted Crisis potential and assessed urgency define the initial State of Threat that the organisation is facing for that Crisis. That State of Threat will change, typically initially grow, as the Crisis emerges.

The best way of classifying and keeping track of the State of Threat and being Crisis-ready, for an organisation or potentially for society, may be a colour-based ("traffic light") or other Threat Level Advisory System, such as those utilised on a large scale for security and terrorism threats.

For example, the US National Terrorism Advisory System (NTAS) is a terrorism threat advisory scale used by the Department of Homeland Security since April 26, 2011, and is the replacement for the often-criticised, colour-coded Homeland Security Advisory System introduced by the George W. Bush administration in 2002. Under this, alerts are issued under one of the three distinct categories of threats of

- Elevated,
- Intermediate, or
- Imminent.

In contrast, in the UK, the Terror Threat Levels, often referred to as UK Threat Levels, are the alert states that have been in use since 1 August 2006 by the British government to warn of forms of terrorist activity. Before this, a colour-based alert scheme known as BIKINI state was used. The current system has the following five threat levels:

- Low — an attack is highly unlikely
- Moderate — an attack is possible but not likely
- Substantial — an attack is likely
- Severe — an attack is highly likely
- Critical — an attack is highly likely in the near future.

In the context of organisational responses to Global Crises, organisations having their own simple classification system for the State of Threat, or a common one similar to the above five-point scale, but parametrised to their own context for a given Global Crisis, would be clearly highly beneficial.

For a major category of Global Crises, Pandemics, the World Health Organisation (WHO) has developed an Influenza Pandemic Phase classification that is partly analogous to a State of Threat classification. The WHO pandemic phases, analogous to States of Threat, were developed in 1999 and revised in 2005, 2009 and 2013. The phases are applicable to the entire world and provide a global framework to aid countries in pandemic preparedness and response planning. The classification has been based on a six-phased approach for easy incorporation into national preparedness and response plans. Phases 1–3 correlate with preparedness, including capacity development and response planning activities, while Phases 4–6 are seen as corresponding to the need for response and mitigation efforts. See Figures 3.4 and 3.5.

In general, especially with Global Crises other than pandemics and, in particular, Black Swan Crises not seen before, the assumed linear path through all States of Threat will not necessarily hold. Instead, the State of Threat identified at the first sighting of the Crisis will change, initially probably growing, as the Crisis emerges. A lot will depend on the Initial Crisis Response at First Sighting and after. We may see continuity or jumps

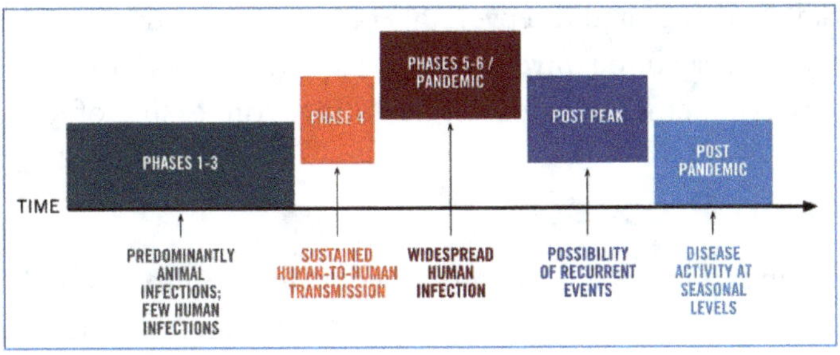

FIGURE 3 PANDEMIC INFLUENZA PHASES (2009)

From: 4. THE WHO PANDEMIC PHASES

Pandemic Influenza Preparedness and Response: A WHO Guidance Document
Geneva: World Health Organization; 2009.

Figure 3.4. WHO Pandemic Influenza Phases, 2009

TABLE 3 WHO PANDEMIC PHASE DESCRIPTIONS AND MAIN ACTIONS BY PHASE

	ESTIMATED PROBABILITY OF PANDEMIC	DESCRIPTION	MAIN ACTIONS IN AFFECTED COUNTRIES	MAIN ACTIONS IN NOT-YET-AFFECTED COUNTRIES
PHASE 1	Uncertain	No animal influenza virus circulating among animals has been reported to cause infection in humans.	Producing, implementing, exercising, and harmonizing national pandemic influenza preparedness and response plans with national emergency preparedness and response plans.	
PHASE 2		An animal influenza virus circulating in domesticated or wild animals is known to have caused infection in humans and is therefore considered a specific potential pandemic threat.		
PHASE 3		An animal or human-animal influenza reassortant virus has caused sporadic cases or small clusters of disease in people, but has not resulted in human-to-human transmission sufficient to sustain community-level outbreaks.		
PHASE 4	Medium to high	Human-to-human transmission of an animal or human-animal influenza reassortant virus able to sustain community-level outbreaks has been verified.	Rapid containment.	Readiness for pandemic response.
PHASE 5	High to certain	The same identified virus has caused sustained community-level outbreaks in at least two countries in one WHO region.	Pandemic response: each country to implement actions as called for in their national plans.	Readiness for imminent response.
PHASE 6	Pandemic in progress	In addition to the criteria defined in Phase 5, the same virus has caused sustained community-level outbreaks in at least one other country in another WHO region.		
POST-PEAK PERIOD		Levels of pandemic influenza in most countries with adequate surveillance have dropped below peak levels.	Evaluation of response; recovery; preparation for possible second wave.	
POSSIBLE NEW WAVE		Level of pandemic influenza activity in most countries with adequate surveillance is rising again.	Response	-
POST-PANDEMIC PERIOD		Levels of influenza have returned to the levels seen for seasonal influenza in most countries with adequate surveillance.	Evaluation of response; revision of plans; recovery.	

From: 4. THE WHO PANDEMIC PHASES

Pandemic Influenza Preparedness and Response: A WHO Guidance Document
Geneva: World Health Organization; 2009.

Figure 3.5. WHO Pandemic Phase Descriptions

between States of Threat and recycling. For example, in the Covid-19 Crisis the potential for second, third, and subsequent, waves potentially worse than the first soon emerged globally, resulting from easing of lockdown.

Monitoring Processes

It follows from the above discussion that constant monitoring of the current State of Threat and indications of changes to this are essential in order to identify both expected and unprecedented changes and respond to them in an effective and timely way. In consequence, the Crisis Response at First Sighting needs to include heightening, or the initiation of active State of Threat monitoring, if this is not already in place.

Crises are multidimensional and complex with a plethora of potential hazards obscuring the emerging threat. Considering the analogous monitoring of terrorism or cyber security threats gives us a framework for considering how to organise for real-time observation and monitoring of initiating sequences and events at national and global, as well as organisational levels. In this context, Gartner defines Threat Intelligence as the following[1]:

> *Threat intelligence is evidence-based knowledge, including context, mechanisms, indicators, implications and actionable advice, about an existing or emerging menace or hazard to assets that can be used to inform decisions regarding the subject's response to that menace or hazard.*

In cyber security, Threat Intelligence has become crucial today because it helps an organisation proactively determine which threats represent the greatest risks to their business. It offers insight into the threats that have, will, or are currently threatening the organisation, its employees and customers. Such threats could potentially lead to the loss of revenue, diminished brand reputation, the destabilisation of operations, and more. Having this knowledge enables the organisation to identify and prioritise the most likely dangers or causes of trouble so they can dedicate their available resources where they will be most effective.

---

[1] https://www.gartner.com/en/documents/2487216/definition-threat-intelligence.

PD CEN/TS 17091:2018 acknowledges that it is important for people at all levels of the organisation to recognise the warning signs and understand that crises can initiate in a number of different ways. However, since PD CEN/TS 17091:2018 does not explicitly treat a Crisis as potentially phased and systemic but instead implicitly treats Crises as point events, it assumes that the ways a Crisis initiates can be summarised in terms of

1. extreme disruptive incidents,
2. poorly managed incidents and business fluctuations, and
3. emergence of latent problems with serious consequences.

It does acknowledge that many Crises have characteristics of more than one type.

In everyday usage, monitoring is typically defined as observing and checking the condition or progress of something or some circumstance over a period of time and keeping it under systematic review. It follows that a monitoring process defines how this is done and in the context of monitoring the current State of Threat, The Intelligence Cycle, as laid out by the Federation of American Scientists (FAS) in the context of US National Security, is defined as the process for developing raw information into finished intelligence for decision makers.[2]

This process has five recurring cyclical steps. See Figure 3.6.

Step 1, 'Planning and Direction', starts with identifying the need for monitoring and progresses to arrangements for delivering threat intelligence to the decision makers. It is the beginning and the end of the cycle — the beginning because it involves drawing up specific collection requirements and the end because delivery of finished intelligence which supports decision-making, may itself generate new requirements.

Step 2, 'Collection', is the gathering of the raw information needed to produce the finished intelligence.

Step 3, 'Processing', involves converting the vast amount of information collected to a form usable by analysts through data reduction.

Step 4, 'All Source Analysis and Production', is the conversion of basic information into finished intelligence. It includes integrating, evaluating,

[2] https://fas.org/irp/cia/product/facttell/intcycle.htm

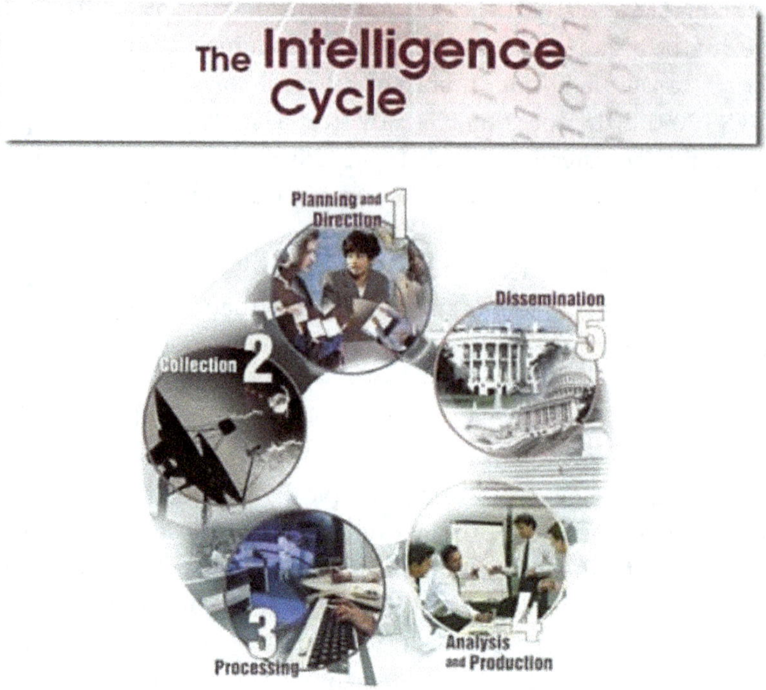

Figure 3.6. The FAS Intelligence Cycle
Source: https://fas.org/irp/cia/product/facttell/intcycle.htm.

and analysing all available data — which is often fragmentary and even contradictory — and preparing intelligence products. Analysts, who are subject-matter specialists, consider the information's reliability, validity, and relevance. They integrate data into a coherent whole, put the evaluated information in context, and produce finished intelligence that includes assessments of events and judgments about the implications of the information for the organisation.

Finally, Step 5, 'Dissemination', is the last step, but logically feeds around again into the first. It is the distribution of the finished intelligence to the decision makers, whose needs initiated the intelligence requirements.

The Intelligence Cycle can be used as a model in the context of organising for monitoring emerging crises. It defines the process steps, roles and functions that need to be addressed. It tells us what we need to do. It is used currently in the context of national security because the need for it there is recognised. However, the recognition of the related need for organisations in the context of Global Crises has, until now, not been by any means fully realised. The consequence of that has been tragic.

Timescales

The exponential behaviour that we recognised in Chapter 1 and earlier in this chapter means that there is a strong danger that, by the time we act in a Crisis, it is already far too late. The accumulating Crisis is then too big to cope with and, in any event, any interventions and containment we introduce will also take time to have any effect.

Explicit consideration of timescales for the emerging Crisis — predicted, likely and/or changing — is hence essential. We need to understand and monitor the urgency, in order to respond effectively. So, monitoring itself needs to include current predictions of timed implications.

There is considerable uncertainty, of course, in predicting timescales for a Crisis, and a strong danger that we underestimate the immediacy and urgency, so that we still take decisive action too late. Accordingly, pessimistic prediction is advised based on the earliest possible entry to the next phase of the Crisis based on current knowledge, with constant updates and revisions to this based on constant observation.

Automating these predictions as part of the monitoring process — especially in Steps 3 and 4 of the Intelligence Cycle — is highly desirable but, as with all automation of key processes within a VUCA (volatile, uncertain, complex and ambiguous) environment, care must be taken to validate the appropriateness of the logic and scope of the automated algorithms and processes. In addition, human oversight is still necessary, since the nature of Crises and the VUCA environment mean that the implicit and explicit assumptions of structure in the automated algorithms and processes may still subsequently become inappropriate due, say, to a Black Swan.

Managing Avoidance, Delay and Mitigation

The responses to a Crisis from the First Sighting onwards may include attempts at avoidance, delay and/or mitigation. Avoidance and mitigation are traditional core strategies of Risk Management, but in the context of an emerging systemic threat, such as a Crisis, delay is also a viable strategy, since it gives additional time for countermeasures, avoidance and mitigation to be effective.

Such delay, albeit for a limited period, is also important in an emerging Crisis as it can provide the opportunity to reduce stress on key containment resources at critical times, such as managing the peak loading demand on hospital beds in the COVID-19 pandemic by delaying infections through social distancing measures.

It follows that from the First Sighting of a Crisis, it is important to manage avoidance, delay and mitigation activities in real time, based on continuous monitoring as the Crisis unfolds. The approach should be a continuous one, with continuous monitoring, rather than waiting for specific points in the development of the Crisis. Because the speed of the development of the Crisis is unknown — at best assumed, speculated or predicted — continuous monitoring and control are crucial for effective Crisis response.

4

Knowing the Crisis Is Here

Introduction

Once a Crisis has arrived and begun to unfold, the mechanisms driving propagation gather momentum and acceleration and there is a need to as quickly as possible evaluate the situation based on real-time information and optimally deploy Crisis protocols.

At what point do the circumstances change from us seeing the Crisis is coming to knowing the Crisis is here? The separation may be artificial, but still important, since both human behaviour and morale will be affected, as well as the immediacy and focus of Crisis response.

This chapter examines management through this initial period of realisation immediately following the arrival of the Crisis. It includes using early warnings and leading indicators, application of clear evaluation and decision criteria, changing human behaviours and organisational objectives, and the deployment of Crisis Protocols.

Of course, the switch over between Crisis phases may not be obvious and clear cut. If we now look back at Figure 3.1, at what point would we decide that the Crisis have actually arrived, and we have swapped from 'Knowing the Crisis is Coming' to 'Knowing the Crisis is Here'?

In part, the response to this rhetorical question is tied up with the exponential nature of the propagation of the Crisis that we have discussed in previous chapters. For example, in the COVID-19 Crisis, after the first domestic cases had been reported the rapid escalation in numbers quickly defined the transition. Accordingly, the first few, indeed one or two, cases could be seen as the transition point although the dissemination of the realisation of the phase change will not be immediate for all.

Despite this, in the context of that example with Covid, the answer is relatively straightforward. The phase transition can be defined as when our coping health care containment resources cannot keep up with demand and are overrun. In general, we know a Crisis is here when we, our organisation, ourself or our society, first feels the real pain, albeit perhaps to start at a low but emerging level.

In this context it is important to make a distinction between the perception of upcoming pain, and the pain itself. Whilst perception or early indicators of upcoming pain — whether its shortages, infection rates, hospital occupancies, cash holdings or anything else — do represent potential impending doom, doom itself will typically be measured by death rates, bankruptcies, economic collapse and serious threat to the sustainment of the existing system.

But the differences can be subtle and depend strongly on the specific definition of each specific Crisis. Crises are multidimensional, and can be seen from various viewpoints, but it's essential to have in place an agreed unambiguous holistic definition of the Crisis to be able to communicate, plan and manage throughout its cycle. Of course, only when we know and agree exactly what the Crisis is, can we say unambiguously whether it's here or not.

Early Warnings and Leading Indicators

Once a Crisis is known to have arrived, we need to understand as well as we can the current reality and act accordingly. Whilst the detail of all we will be facing as the Crisis unfolds is likely to still be far from clear, there will be early warnings and leading indicators of what is still to come.

Accordingly, at this shift of phase in the Crisis lifecycle, it is appropriate to review and, as appropriate, reconfirm or reimagine and replan, both the deployed infrastructure of our Crisis Management System and the information and analysis to date of the situation and its likely development and alternative scenarios. Such review, reconfirmation, replanning and reimagining needs to be timely, holistic, focused and extensive.

Early warnings of how the Crisis will further unfold will primarily be of two types. These reflect respectively insights into the characteristics and dimensions of the unfolding Crisis, and insights into its parameters of spread, speed and acceleration.

Considering firstly using early warnings in terms of the characteristics and dimensions of the unfolding Crisis, these may come in many forms and in addressing these it is crucially important to consider the Big Picture, taking account of the potential interrelationships between the parameters and variables that characterise the Crisis.

Since 'Knowing the Crisis is Here' involves recognising that coping resources can no longer keep up with demand and will typically be measured by death rates, bankruptcies, economic collapse and serious threat to the sustainment of the existing system, examples of early warnings in terms of the characteristics and dimensions of the unfolding Crisis are, for example, when a perhaps unforeseen but serious consequence or domino effect is first identified as potentially already in progress.

Thus, the financial implications of the COVID-19 Crisis partially emerged as the Crisis propagated. For example, as part of the OECD Policy Responses to COVID-19, a paper on 'The impact of the coronavirus (COVID-19) crisis on development finance' in June 2020 identified that:

> *The current global context ... risks a significant reduction in the financing available to developing economies. In sum, external private finance inflows to developing economies could drop by USD 700 billion in 2020 compared to 2019 levels, exceeding the immediate impact of the 2008 Global Financial Crisis by 60%. This exacerbates the risk of major development setbacks that would, in turn, increase our vulnerability to future pandemics, climate change and other global public bads.*[1]

Such an early warning is a call to action. Early warning calls to action arise, with proper monitoring, at all levels, organisational, national and global. And it is important to the management of the Crisis at whatever level, that they do result in coherent joined-up, thought-through, holistic and planned action.

Unfortunately, alas, they often do not. Responses are often seen as piecemeal and reflecting a desperate desire to catch-up. They may overreact

[1] http://www.oecd.org/coronavirus/policy-responses/the-impact-of-the-coronavirus-covid-19-crisis-on-development-finance-9de00b3b/.

and precipitate further damage and unintended consequences. This, of course, has been a criticism at the national level globally throughout the COVID-19 Crisis.

Avoiding any such hindsight and outcome bias, a 'Control Room' approach to Crisis management does offer an opportunity for more coherent joined-up, thought-through, holistic and planned action, but given the phased nature of Crises we have discussed, this presupposes the existence of a dynamic ongoing 'Risk Management Control Room' rather than a temporary short cycle 'Business Continuity Control Room'.

And a Horizon Scanning approach to identify the characteristics and dimensions of the unfolding Crisis needs to be taken, with an emphasis on potential interconnectivities and the Big Picture as well as the implications of the Volatile, Uncertain, Complex and Ambiguous (VUCA) environment.

The other form of early warning concerns insights into various parameters of spread, speed and acceleration of the unfolding Crisis. Here, the concerning insights are typically those of serious escalation necessitating, once again, appropriate calls to action. The 'R number' used extensively in the COVID-19 pandemic is a good example. See Figure 4.1. In this case, the R number is a leading indicator of the COVID-19 Crisis that provides early warning of the Crisis' progression since it measures infection rates, not direct demand on the coping hospital resources (Figure 4.2).

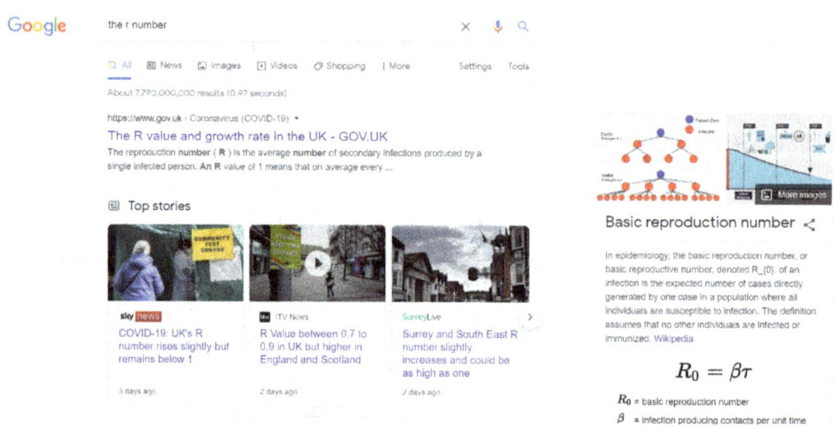

Figure 4.1. Extract from Google 'The R Number' March 2021

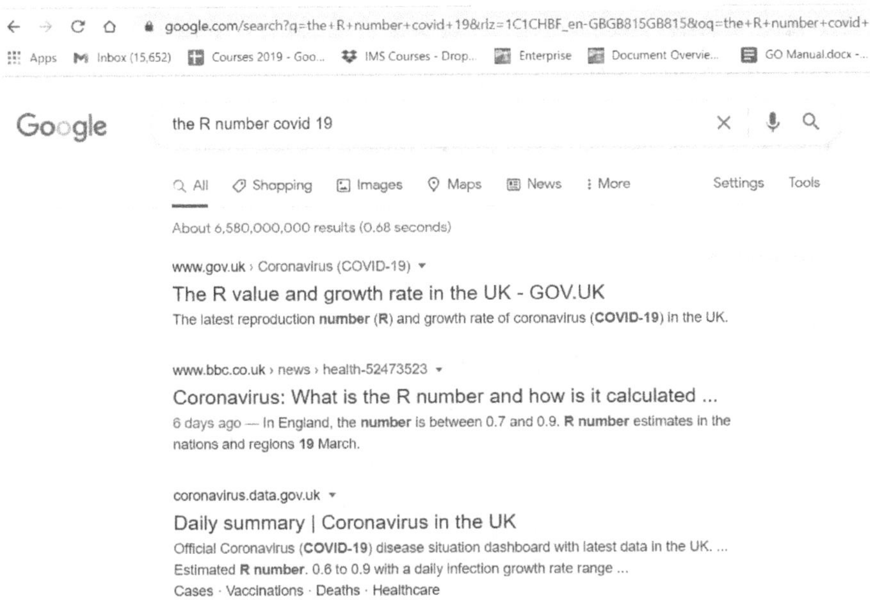

Figure 4.2. Extract from Google 'The R Number COVID-19' March 2021

The R number has become so much a part of the monitoring of the pandemic that Google identifies some 7,790 million results in searching for the term. But the R number is not just for description, the level of the R number and changes in its value trigger changes in government responses to the pandemic. Analogously, the levels of, and changes in, appropriate leading indicators at global, national or organisational level should form the basis for changes in organisational responses to the unfolding Crisis.

Further, where we are using a clearly defined leading indicator such as the R number, pre-set warning and/or action levels for that indicator can be established to automate initiation of additional review or action as the Crisis reaches key levels. See Figure 4.3.

Nevertheless, it is important not to see a single indicator in isolation, or a limited set, as the sole indicators of the Crisis. The R number does not deal with severity of cases nor how many are currently infected. See Figure 4.4. For COVID-19, these three indicators together might be called 'the big 3' indicators, but other indicators may also be important such as the extent

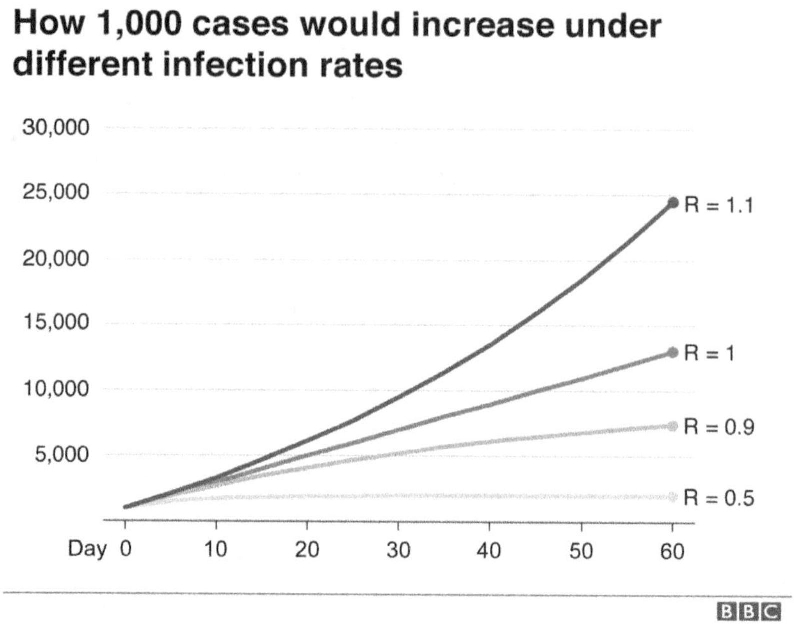

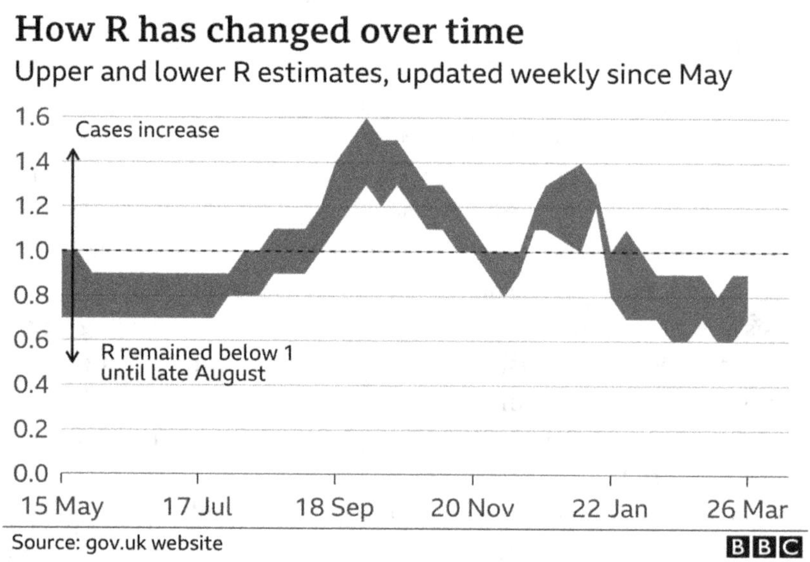

Figure 4.3. The Effect of the R Number

Source: BBC News 'Coronavirus: What is the R number and how is it calculated?,' https://www.bbc.co.uk/news/health-52473523, accessed 30th March 2021.

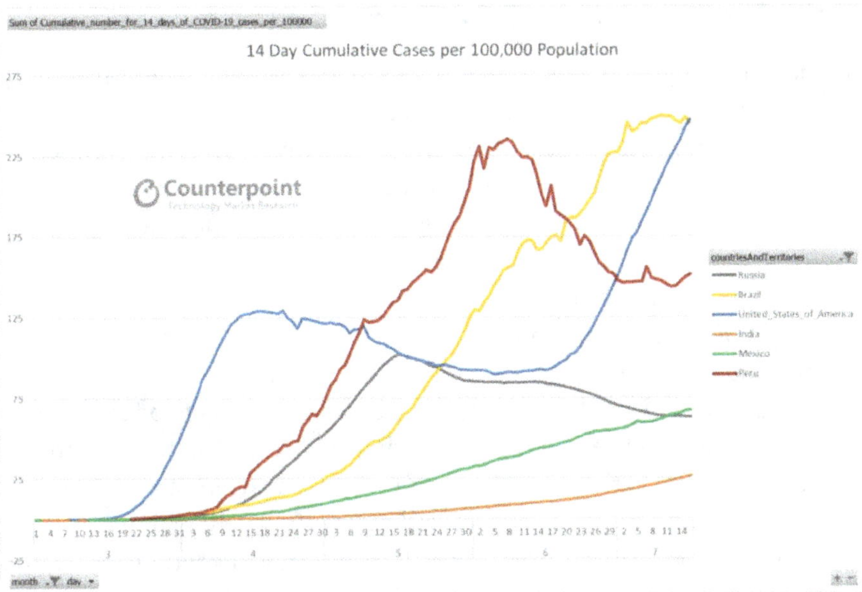

Figure 4.4. COVID-19 Update Week 29

Source: 'Weekly Update: Global Coronavirus Impact and Implications' March 25, 2021, https://www.counterpointresearch.com/coronavirus-weekly-update/.

of vaccination, the speed at which infection occurs or infection rates in key at-risk groups likely to need hospitalisation. We need an appropriate inclusive set of leading indicators.

Clearly, it is important that both early warnings in terms of the characteristics and dimensions of the unfolding Crisis, and in terms of leading indicators of its parameters of spread, speed and acceleration, are reviewed at the arrival of the Crisis. Either set alone is inadequate.

Leading indicators can be misleading taken in isolation and possibly out of context; they are typically based on implicit assumptions and may ignore key aspects or developments. Considering the characteristics and dimensions of the Crisis helps put this in context.

Conversely, focusing on the potentially expanding characteristics and dimensions of the unfolding Crisis, still requires us to be fully conscious of speed. So, we need to be alert for new dimensions and for changes of pace.

Clear Evaluation and Decision Criteria

Decision making processes within organisations are often not fully transparent and clear, involve some aspects of stakeholder alignment and, especially in the context of 'difficult decisions' involving conflicting objectives and needs, may be time consuming and problematic.

Once an individual or a group within an organisation faces an issue requiring decision making, alternative decision outcomes should be identified and evaluated objectively before settling on a choice. The goal is to compare the options before coming to a decision on the most advantageous solution.

In practice, however, it is difficult for decision-makers to be completely objective in their choice and frequently they will select the solution that is the most satisfying to them. So, decision making has an emotional element.

Further, sometimes we make decisions instinctively or intuitively by comparing situations that arise with those we have experienced before, thereby speeding up the process. Intuition allows us to find solutions without consciously using logical or analytical reasoning, so using your intuition could be an effective shortcut if used well.

To complicate matters further, in group decision-making decision-makers each have their own interests, or those of their group, to defend. The decision-making process then takes the form of a negotiation between decision-makers who may defend their positions according to their needs or pet subjects.

When a situation is complex and it's difficult to know all the elements involved, it might come down to making a quick decision, while accepting the uncertainty and the consequential risks tied to it. Even in normal circumstances, that requires quite a bit of courage.

Whilst making good, fast decisions is challenging under the best of circumstances, the trickiest are the so-called 'big bets'; unfamiliar, high-stakes decisions. When you have the extreme uncertainty of a Crisis, such as we saw in the COVID-19 pandemic, which arrived with enormous speed and considerable scale, organizations can face a potentially paralyzing volume of these big-bet decisions.

Typically, when a Crisis occurs, whether it's economic, health, political or otherwise, the balance within the organisation's systems needs to be readjusted, often abruptly. During such crises, when faced with too much information or with uncertainty, people are forced to simplify their mental patterns unconsciously so as to make quick decisions. The consequential intuitive mode of operation is, however, more vulnerable to reasoning bias.

McKinsey argued in March 2020 that 'unprecedented crises demand unprecedented actions' and that lessons from past crises suggest that leaders of organisations are more likely to underreact than overact. They suggested that 'it is necessary in such circumstances to take the bold and rapid actions that would feel too risky in normal times.'

The issue here is that the typically many organisations, big and small, are far too slow at decision making to be able keep up in such turbulence. Postponing decisions to wait for more information might make sense during usual circumstances, but when the environment is uncertain — and defined by urgency and imperfect information — waiting to decide is a potentially dangerous decision in itself.

In 'normal' circumstances, delaying a decision or avoiding making one, may be viable strategies since the continuation of the status quo is a viable possibility, at least in the short term. In Crises, the speed of acceleration makes gaps in effective decision making potentially lethal.

When the Crisis is already rolling out, there is a pressing need, and very little time, to make key decisions. So, ahead of this when we can see the Crisis coming, decision making processes should be reviewed, reimagined and streamlined to ensure that decisions that will need to be made under Crisis conditions are well-based and timely. A key element here is assuring the availability of pertinent, correct and timely information for decision making.

There is a link here also to ongoing monitoring and review, and to arrangements for Business Continuity. Continuous observation and review are ideal in such Crisis circumstances, and arrangements for managing Business Continuity should have been planned to integrate responsively with these pre-set monitoring and review arrangements.

But preparation should have started much earlier in other dimensions also. As many decisions as possible, certainly the predictable decisions that we know will need to be made as the Crisis unfolds, should have been made earlier, when we could see it coming before it started. Or, at least, preliminary decisions that will stand unless unexpected variation takes place in the rollout of the Crisis. For example, we can plan at what point we will trigger various copping emergency measures, such as reducing physical contact and increasing virtual.

For those decisions still left to be made during the Crisis itself, typically critical to minimising the pain as well as survival and recovery, it is necessary to plan for appropriately safe and speedy decision making in potentially unstable and volatile conditions.

The typical VUCA characteristics of our modern environment-volatility, uncertainty, complexity and ambiguousness-become all the more prevalent in a Crisis and one clear lesson from the COVID-19 Pandemic has been that there have been numerous erroneous decisions made at both government and organisational levels under such Crisis conditions. These, alas, add to the management pressure and may propagate the Crisis further.

Accordingly, there is a clear need to ensure that as simple as possible evaluation criteria are established in advance for all decisions likely to need to be made during the Crisis rollout. The simpler the criteria, the easier also to keep them under constant monitoring and review. Some of these evaluation criteria will typically be for 'trigger decisions', whereby actions regarded as inevitable, but preferably delayable, will be instigated.

Crisis Protocols

Protocols for the conduct of management before and during the Crisis are referred to throughout this book. The context in this section, however, is specifically on real-time management processes during the unfolding of the Crisis.

We previously discussed Crisis Management Systems and the concept of the Crisis Control Room. In this context, what Crisis Protocols should there be to come into force as the Crisis initiates?

Whilst a lot of guidance can come from existing Business Continuity protocols, these often have limited scope, focus almost exclusively on operational resilience and do not necessarily deal with the holistic context, extensiveness and hence organisational strategic issues associated with a systemic Global Crisis. They can also mistakenly treat a Crisis as a point event, rather than an emergent unfolding escalating process. Plus, unfortunately many organisations have multiple, not-joined-up, Business Continuity plans.

Arguably, the most important aspect of Crisis Protocols as the Crisis unfolds is around the need to make decisions and consequential deployment of resultant actions. Accordingly, the necessary protocol needs to ensure that we remain clear and focused on purpose and achievable goals; we are aware of foreseeable and evolving risks and plausible scenarios; we stay aware, agile and responsive; we listen to our intuition and keep our emotions under appropriate controls; we focus on avoiding decision biases; we work together as a team with common goals rather than as competing adversaries; and we communicate well and move forward, even if that means fixing things afterwards.

There is also a need to both scan the horizon and challenge all the usual assumptions of 'business as usual', and to keep challenging these on a cyclical basis throughout the Crisis. We should keep questioning ourselves and our colleagues and teams with questions such as:

- How might things unfold from here?
- What is most important right now?
- What might we be missing?
- What could we influence now that could pay off later?

Reliable and timely information acquisition in a Crisis is crucial. It could be said that for this reason McKinsey argues that during crises we should involve more people in the decision-making process. They argue that during the uncertainty of a Crisis, leaders often wish to limit decision making to those at the top of the organisation, with a small team making the big decisions 'behind closed doors'. McKinsey argue that organisational leaders should reject the hierarchical model that they might be more comfortable with in normal times and instead involve many more stakeholders and encourage different views and debate. This approach they believe can lead to smarter decisions without sacrificing speed.

McKinsey specifically suggest a 'Fishbowl Model' as in Figure 4.5 in which decision makers and key experts sit around an actual, or virtual, table in order to make decisions. Sitting at the table are one or two decision makers and multiple experts, as well as one or two 'empty seats' for other relevant stakeholders in the gallery to rotate into, as they have points to share. Meanwhile, the majority of stakeholders observe the meeting, which

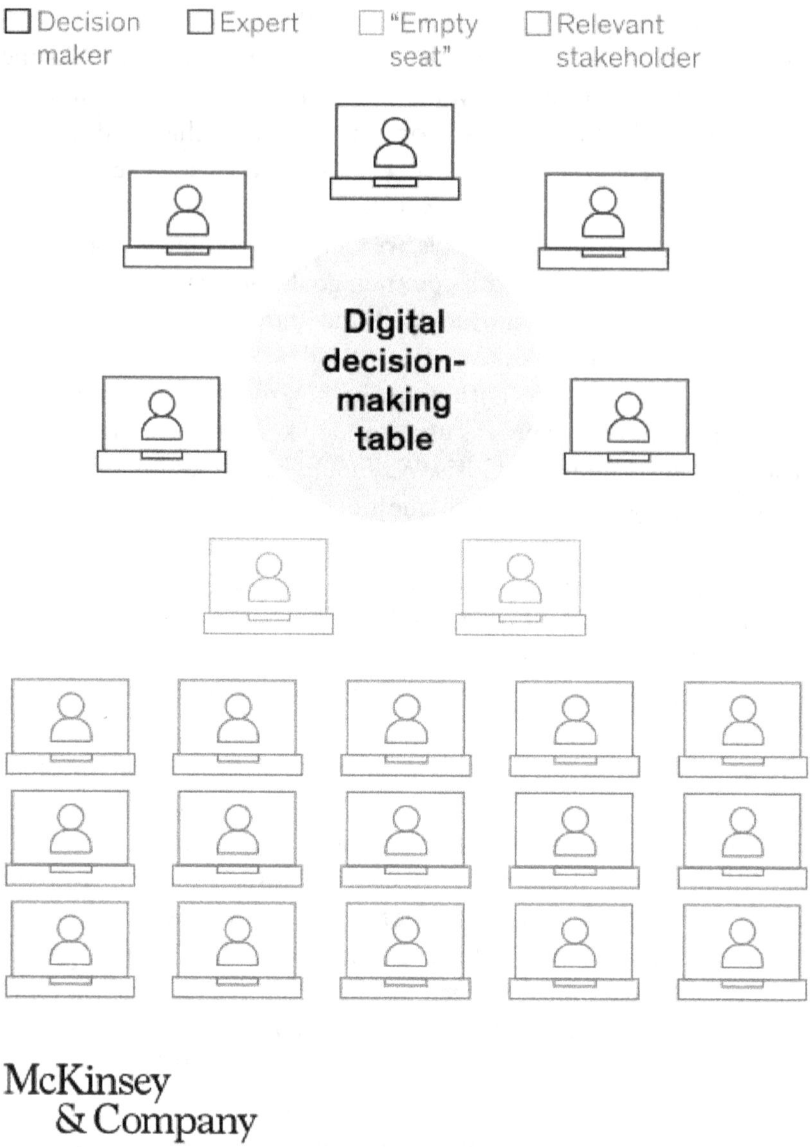

Figure 4.5. The Fishbowl Format

Source: Decision making in uncertain times, McKinsey March 24, 2020, https://www.mckinsey.com/business-functions/organization/our-insights/decision-making-in-uncertain-times.

builds understanding, without having to make an extra communication step afterward.

In an in-person meeting, stakeholders watching the Fishbowl can contribute information and ideas by temporarily taking one of the empty seats and briefly participating in the meeting, and then returning to the gallery. In a virtual meeting, the stakeholders are on mute but can participate by 'raising their hand,' with a moderator inviting them in and unmuting them.

In this context, McKinsey suggests that leaders can involve more people by:

1. First clarifying the decisions to be made.
2. Identifying only a small number of decision makers.
3. Identifying which stakeholders need to have a voice, including relevant experts, and those who will be responsible for implementing decisions.
4. Creating a forum for rapid debate to take place, where everyone has a voice, but not necessarily a vote.

It is possible to involve a large number of stakeholders and experts within this approach without sacrificing speed. It is based on the idea that in VUCA times when the decisions you may be making are bold, you need many points of view to make sure the decision makers aren't missing something.

The challenge of decision making is a lot to expect from a protocol, so it is important that these matters are thought through well in advance of the Crisis initiating and that the resultant protocol is appropriate, up to date and ready to initiate. In common with Business Continuity planning, we should not just prepare in advance, but also run tabletop, functional and full-scale exercises based on the Crisis Protocol.

Such tabletop exercises may be simulated sessions with organisational staff members meeting informally in a meeting room to walk through events, roles and responses in one or more particular Crisis scenarios. Typically, a facilitator is used to guide participants and the duration depends on the audience, the topic being exercised and the exercise objectives. Many tabletop exercises can be conducted in a few hours, so such exercises can be cost-effective tools to validate protocols, plans and capabilities.

Functional exercises allow organisational personnel to validate Crisis protocols, plans and readiness by performing their Crisis roles in a simulated scenario-driven Crisis environment, such as the failure of a critical business function or a specific hazard scenario. Typically, functional exercises are designed to exercise specific personnel, protocols and resources which may include communications, warning, notifications and equipment set-up.

A full-scale exercise is as close to a real Crisis as possible, again in a simulated scenario-driven environment. Multiple functional groups, partner organisations and others may be involved. Typically, therefore, this is a lengthy exercise using, as much as possible, the equipment and personnel that would be called upon in the real Crisis.

Changing Objectives & Behaviour

As we saw during the COVID-19 Pandemic, we, and our organisations, can change dramatically when faced with an unfolding Crisis. Organisations that were heavily shareholder-value focused, driven by financial requirements and targets, suddenly were transformed into a varying dual emphasis on surviving the Crisis themselves, and supporting their customer, employees and society. For example, organisations shifted to local production and supply of scarce key personal protective equipment (PPE) and medically related equipment, sometimes on a no-profit basis.

Crises can bring out the good and bad in us and our organisations. But, more importantly, they do rightly change our objectives and behaviour. Sticking to pre-crisis objectives slavishly in a Crisis can be a path to ruin and oblivion. With good leadership, and good leaders, the ability to swiftly recognise the circumstances and transform the organisational imperatives is a key to survival. But, even better that this **agility**, the ability to **foresee** the potential need to do this, and **plan** accordingly, is even more important.

Thus, when the Crisis has arrived, the review and establishment of objectives needs to take place speedily as a routine planned activity, rather than as an exception. The assumption of ongoing continuity of organisational objectives needs to be avoided, other than until this speedy review has taken place. Emergency business continuity arrangements need to incorporate this refocusing arrangement, rather than implicitly assuming 'objectives as usual'.

Human behaviour, of the organisation's employees, needs to be refocused also. In a Crisis, the employee's duty of care implicit in operations and human interfaces becomes larger. So, an increased awareness of customer and colleagues needs, and responsibility for protecting and supporting them, becomes needed. Timely and appropriate management communication and training is important to support this. So again, foresight, planning, communication, and agility are key enablers.

But, what about the organisational culture to support this, and the leadership to make it happen? An organisational culture and leadership not just based on 'business as usual', but on flexibility, foresight and agility is needed.

5

Organisational Management Through the Crisis

Introduction

Once underway, the Crisis will be seen as having its own momentum, and in some organisations, Business Continuity and/or Emergency Management will come into play. Business Continuity is an essential aspect of response to a Global Crisis, protecting the organisation, its customers and other stakeholders.

The main Business Continuity Management international standard is ISO 22301: 2019 'Security and resilience — Business continuity management systems — Requirements'. This defines Business Continuity for an organisation as its capability to continue the delivery of its products and services within acceptable time frames at a predefined capacity **during a disruption**. Note the limiting emphasis on operations.

The standard in turn defines **disruption** as an anticipated or unanticipated **incident** that causes an unplanned, negative deviation from the expected delivery of products and services according to the organisation's objectives. Finally, an **incident** is defined, a little circularly, as an event that can be, or could lead to, a disruption, loss, emergency or crisis. While an event is not explicitly defined within the standard, it is immediately evident that the usage reflects the previously identified lack of emphasis on the sequential phases of Crises.

ISO 22301: 2019 specifies the structure and requirements for implementing and maintaining a Business Continuity Management System (BCMS) that can appropriately support business continuity following a disruption. The organisation's size and structure, its legal, regulatory and industry requirements, as well as its products and services provided, processes employed, sector and the requirements of its interested parties, affect the outcomes of maintaining a BCMS. However, a BCMS is an essential requirement for effective and efficient organisational management through a Crisis.

In putting in place a BCMS, it is necessary to establish appropriate business continuity policies and objectives based on an understanding of the organisation's needs and that of its stakeholders. Business Continuity processes need to be identified, established, operated and maintained. In addition, there is a need to define and provide capabilities and response structures for ensuring the organisation will survive disruptions and put in place monitoring and review of the performance and effectiveness of the BCMS as well as its continual improvement.

An important issue, however, in many organisations, including those pursuing ERM, is that the integration of Business Continuity Management with the allegedly holistic organisational Enterprise Risk Management framework is often limited. Furthermore, limitations of the underlying static nature of the model may mean that real-time planning and control are also limited in scope. This chapter considers the issues, implications, and remedies, for management through the Crisis.

It also includes three case study examples of good practice in managing the COVID-19 Crisis from organisations across the World. While typically even the best, most excellent organisations have not responded to the recent COVID-19 Crisis particularly well, and not fully coherently, and there are many horror stories of very poor organisational responses, there are also some outstandingly good responses in relation to particular aspects. For example, it can be said that the Abu Dhabi Police, and BLUEBELLA and Nottingham City Council in the UK, all demonstrated exceptional responsiveness to the dynamic challenging circumstances of the Crisis. With this in mind, this chapter also includes case study material on good practices from real organisations.

Business Continuity and Emergency Management

There are a variety of other applicable international standards covering specific aspects in the broad area of Business Continuity, as well as ISO 22301: 2019. These include the following:

- PD ISO/TS 22330 Guidelines for people aspects of business continuity
- PD ISO/TS 22318 Guidelines for supply chain continuity
- ISO 22313 Security and resilience — Business continuity management systems — Guidance on the use of ISO 22301
- ISO 22316 Security and resilience — Organisational resilience — Principles and attributes
- ISO 22320 Security and resilience — Emergency management — Guidelines for incident management
- ISO 22395 Security and resilience — Community resilience — Guidelines for supporting vulnerable persons in an emergency
- ISO 22319 Security and resilience — Community resilience — Guidelines for planning the involvement of spontaneous volunteers
- BS 67000 City resilience — Guide

Business Continuity Management is more than just Emergency Management, since continuity of operations can be an issue in non-emergency circumstances also, and we are interested in more than just an Emergency Response. Typically, Emergency Response focuses on the safety and protection of life, assets, and the environment. On the other hand, Business Continuity focuses on continuing the operations of the business until it can return back to normal.

Thus, Emergency Management seeks to safeguard people from harm, while Business Continuity is focused on the continuity of key business operations and maintaining or restoring the organisation to its pre-crisis state. Clearly, in a Global Crisis, we potentially need both.

Moreover, whilst Business Continuity will be an ongoing planned but changing requirement, throughout the phases of a Global Crisis, the need for Emergency Management in contrast may be more sporadic, arising at certain points in the Crisis and then dissipating. These points need to be anticipated, monitored and prepared for and Emergency Response needs to be concise, timely and agile.

So, while in an ideal corporate set-up, Emergency Management and Business Continuity teams and personnel could be completely separated from each other, provided that there is full communication and cooperation between them, unfortunately, in real organisations, these roles often get lumped together based on the misguided notion that they are one and the same.

In terms of day to day activities, Emergency Preparedness and Business Continuity involve very distinct tasks:

- Emergency Response often involves directing people and resources away from danger, holding emergency drills and training sessions, evacuating facilities and working with first responders to ensure all stakeholders make it through an emergency safe and sound.
- Business continuity tasks include protecting the business' reputation online, establishing and maintaining redundant systems and support teams, restoring IT systems and ensuring employees are able to return to their daily work tasks following an emergency.

It follows that since Emergency Preparedness and Business Continuity have different goals and activities, the way each of these two functions prepare for a Crisis should arguably be very distinct.

Emergency Preparedness staff must assess all the possible emergencies that could hit their organisation and hold regular team drills or exercises to ensure that the entire business is aware of these threats and knows what to do appropriately in the case of each emergency. They also need to establish how they will effectively distribute the emergency response plans, contact lists and other key documents to employees and other stakeholders.

In contrast, the Business Continuity team may develop plans to mitigate, avoid or minimise the full impact of potential business-disrupting problems. Typically, such Business Continuity Plans are not distributed across the entire organisation but only to identified key stakeholders who should be involved in business continuity efforts. This might include the executive team, the IT department, HR, PR and communications, and other related groups.

So, Business Continuity Management is distinct from, but may in a sense be seen to include, Emergency Management. Clearly though, Emergency Management alone is not enough. Waiting for the next emergency to emerge or suddenly appear during the Crisis, before taking predetermined containment action, is not a viable option. A proactive planned and more holistic approach is required. Putting out sporadic fires does not end the firestorm, however well each fire is put out, and focusing on that can mean our resources are not conserved for what becomes the real survival need.

Organisations being prepared for emergencies are not, therefore, the same as, nor adequate for, being prepared for Global Crises, with their phased structure. In reality, the disconnect between Emergency Management and Business Continuity Management within an organisation can unfortunately be considerable, with inadequate communication, collaboration and alignment in terms of both planning and deployment.

As we discussed in Chapter 2, there is today also unfortunately often a disconnect between Risk Management, which is seen largely as a high-level analytical and planning activity, and Business Continuity Management which involves the planning and discharge of real-time operational response to a Crisis.

Limitations of Current Enterprise Risk Management

In real organisational practice, the integration of Business Continuity Management with the allegedly holistic organisational Enterprise Risk Management framework is often limited.

As we discussed in the Preface, over the last two decades, the desire for a coherent holistic approach to risk across an organisation has been the basis for the emergence of Enterprise Risk Management (ERM) as a new management discipline that calls for companies to identify all the risks they face, to decide which risks to manage actively, and then to make that plan of action available to all stakeholders, rather than just shareholders, as part of their annual reporting. Risk is seen not just as upcoming threats but also in terms of opportunities that may balance them. The release of the Committee of Sponsoring Organisations (COSOs) ERM Integrated Framework in 2004 did much to establish ERM, and it has now become a business school/MBA discipline.

But typically, Business Continuity is not explicitly identified as a component of ERM. Interestingly though, PWC argues that Organisations that integrate Enterprise Risk Management into their strategic planning efforts have found that Business Continuity Management enhances both their value creation objectives and their protection objectives. See Figure 5.1. They say that the confidence that comes from identifying and appropriately addressing interruption risks enables them to more boldly execute those strategic plans. However, they argue that gaining that confidence requires the melding of the ERM and Business Continuity Management programs.

PWC explains that the need to define, create, maintain, and improve an organisation's Business Continuity Management capability often arises from what they call a 'singular event'. This may be, say, a past close call that identified the need for, or increased awareness that, Business Continuity Management improvement was needed. Alternatively, a new regulatory obligation, either directly applied or strongly encouraged by a key customer, might have led to efforts to improve and document recoverability capabilities, or a growing number of cyber threats may have been the catalyst for improving both Business Continuity Management and Emergency Management capabilities.

However, regardless of how the Business Continuity Management program gained its initial traction, its development from a narrow focus has likely resulted in wide gaps in its ability to protect operations and the organisation's operational and strategic goals. PWC have found that it is far less common for an organisation to holistically view its resiliency and recoverability needs from the perspective of managing interruption risk to align with strategic and operational strategies. They say that better risk insight emerges and is optimally addressed when ERM and Business Continuity Management programs are aligned.

Symptoms of misaligned Business Continuity Management and ERM programs that reduce programme effectiveness are common and include the following:

- Separate ERM and Business Continuity Management steering committees and supervision leading to Business Continuity Management programmes that don't address key strategic risks and are too narrowly focused on tactical execution risks.

Figure 5.1. Enterprise Risk Management and ERM

Source: PwC 2020 'Enterprise risk management and business continuity management: Together at last', https://www.pwc.com/us/en/risk-assurance-services/publications/assets/pwc-erm-and-bcm-together-at-last.pdf accessed on 29th April 2021.

- Business Continuity efforts only addressing risks of importance to a subset of the organisation (e.g., IT, supply chain, customer experience, and regulatory compliance), leaving other important interruption impact areas unaddressed.

- The impact of relevant interruption risks on enterprise strategies not being identified punctually because Business Continuity Management does not share ERM's senior leadership visibility.
- Business Continuity recovery strategies contain approaches that are misaligned with enterprise strategy, such as reliance on decentralised operating locations, when centralisation strategies are being executed.
- Business Continuity exercise scenarios do not address critical or emerging interruption risks that the ERM program has already identified.
- Business Continuity Management-identified operational resiliency improvements are not informed by ERM-facilitated management risk tolerance decisions.
- ERM risk assessments are not informed by Business Continuity Management-enabled resiliency and recovery capabilities.
- Business Continuity Management-identified third-party resiliency risks are neither fully communicated to the ERM program nor integrated with overall third-party risk management.
- ERM risk scenario analysis does not consider the entirety of an interruption event's impact and scope, which is typically described in the Business Continuity Management program's business impact analysis.
- Separate ERM and Business Continuity Management program effectiveness reporting to senior management may provide incomplete and disconnected views of the organisation's resiliency and recovery capabilities.
- Inconsistent use of ERM and Business Continuity Management risk taxonomies (i.e., impact categories/thresholds and risk appetite/acceptance) reduces the effectiveness of aggregating, normalising and monitoring risk across the organisation.
- Disconnected ERM and Business Continuity Management program management emphasis reduces the effectiveness of risk identification and response.
- Management fatigue from numerous and disconnected risk assessments results in gaps in assessment coverage and misinterpretation of results.

Real-time Planning and Control Away from the Static Risk Model

Even apart from the issue of lack of integration of Business Continuity Management, the underlying explicit, or more normally implicit, assumption of the static nature of Risk referred to previously, unfortunately, means that an organisation's real-time management through a Global Crisis is anyway limited in scope. And, since a typical meaning for 'Management' is 'Planning and Control', it follows that only a limited scope of planning and control is possible.

The scope that is possible is based on the false assumption of Static Risk, that the risks associated with the initiating, emerging, maturing and resolving Crisis do not evolve or change through this process. If it was safe to be able to make such an assumption, it would greatly simplify organisational management through the Crisis. But, of course, it is very far from safe to do so. Risks do not stay static through a Global Crisis; they change dramatically in real time. So, 'averaging out' risk in that way is severely misleading and extremely dangerous, as it distorts decision-making and urgent actions and responses.

Nevertheless, usually, such an assumption is made implicitly, by treating a Crisis as a point event in the Risk Register. While this risk may be updated from time to time, normally it is reviewed and, in particular, updated too infrequently and with a lag.

The consequence of this is that the management process through the Crisis is theoretically much simpler but inherently inadequate, as successive human empirically based interventions are needed but unfortunately are identified, decided on, and take place, too late. This may have taken place anyway due to the speed of the propagation of the Crisis, but the effect is magnified enormously by ignoring the dynamic phased nature of the risks.

So, how do we move away from this static risk model to real-time planning and control through the Crisis? Before we consider remedies and solutions, we need to first discuss the context, formulation and implications. Moving to a view of a Crisis as a Dynamic Emergent Phased Process, rather than treating it as a point event, has serious implications, particularly when we take account of the realisation that such Crises are normal in a so-called VUCA environment, such as we have today.

The concept of the Volatile, Uncertain, Complex and Ambiguous (VUCA) environment was first recognised in 1987 and has had increased usage since the early 2000s. Such volatility, uncertainty, complexity and ambiguity are now part of the globalised world, with the ever-present potential for disruption becoming more prevalent due to technology and increased communication. The COVID-19 Pandemic and previous Crises, such as the Global Financial Crisis and Iceland volcano, illustrate this reality.

The dynamics of global society, including the globalised economy, place new demands and present new challenges to all organisations. The COVID-19 global pandemic is the latest, but not the only, Crisis to highlight a number of shortcomings with the existing risk frameworks. Issues were already apparent following the Financial Crisis in 2009, as well as previous global and localised Crises and events. It quickly became apparent that the existing risk models failed to help organisations prepare for, or manage through, the immediate crisis and the resulting 'new normal'.

2020 and 2021 have seen the global community collectively experience unprecedented social and economic upheaval in the form of the COVID-19 coronavirus. The true impact of the global pandemic may not become apparent for a number of years, but it is already clear that it has permanently impacted the way we work and live our lives. The organisations, and indeed national economies, that adapt fastest to meet not only these challenges but also opportunities presented will be the ones that shape the 'new normal'.

A fundamental paradigm shift is necessary to appreciate that turbulence and disruption within the global ecosystems are normal not exceptional. Despite being potentially mislead by periods of relative stability, the world today is in constant flux and, to thrive, organisations must be prepared to not only react to external changes but also to actively seek and gain strength from disruption. Risk management needs to reflect this new paradigm.

Learning from the past, organisations need to recognise that the future will be a succession of 'new normals', each with unique challenges and opportunities, and ensure they are simultaneously robust enough to withstand the shocks, agile enough to react, and flexible enough to recognise and exploit new opportunities. Risk Management can no longer be against a backdrop of stability.

Specifically, it can be argued convincingly that today

- exceptions are now Part of Normal,
- we need to be able to properly manage Swans and Rhinos,
- the 'New Normal' Is actually 'a Cascade of New Normals',
- organisations need to become more than Agile; they need to be Anti-Fragile, actually growing in strength from being stressed,
- the Focus on 'Organisational Value' is now bigger than before.

Remedies and Solutions

It follows from the above discussion that there are six key aspects to be considered in redefining and reimagining good Organisational Management through a Global Crisis, in order to ensure its relevance and effectiveness. These are the following:

1. The recognition that every dimension of Organisational Management today must be explicitly Risk-based needs to be holistically strengthened in all aspects, since Risks are now more dynamic, complex and potentially global.
2. A holistic, fully integrated concept of, and approach to, Organisational Risk Management is required, incorporating Business Continuity Management. The false disjointness needs to end.
3. Risk and Organisational Risk Management in the context of Crises need to be based on a phased dynamic model, rather than being treated as point events, similar to the local risks faced by the organisation and included in its Risk Register.
4. The historic paradigm of Organisational Risk and Risk Management being implicitly based on a historically more stable world needs to be replaced by explicit recognition of the VUCA environment, including phenomena, such as Black Swans, Grey Rhinos and Cascading New Normals. This implies an associated reimagining of more dynamic organisational objectives, risks and opportunities and a more continuous approach to Risk awareness, planning and control.
5. Local organisational solutions to Management through a Global Crisis need to reflect the above conceptual remedies for our ailing Risk

Management approach. An approach which is the best we have so far but is grossly inadequate.

6. As with the correct interpretation of the current Risk Management approach, as embedded in ISO 31000, each organisation needs to look at Risk specifically in the specific context of their own organisation and not 'lift' or 'transfer' parts of their Risk Management System from other organisations.

Case Studies

As we said at the beginning of this chapter, while typically even the best, most excellent organisations have not responded to the recent COVID-19 crisis particularly well, and not fully coherently, and there are many horror stories of very poor organisational responses, there are also some outstandingly good responses in relation to particular aspects. Here, we consider three illustrative case study examples of good practice and business agility in managing the COVID-19 Crisis from organisations across the World.

The Abu Dhabi Police

The UAE and Abu Dhabi Emirate Governments have long placed emphasis on business agility as highly important in the conduct of Government entities. To an extent, this has placed government entities in good positions of readiness to respond to the COVID Crisis.

The Abu Dhabi Police GHQ is a leading government entity, whose leadership pays exceptional attention to enhancing its ability to respond rapidly, manage security events, and adapt to and address sudden crises, in a geographical area of more than 67,340 km^2, representing 87% of the country's area. The Abu Dhabi Police leadership, led by H.E. Commander-in-Chief and H.E. Director-General, and the Directors of Sectors, Directorates and Police Departments, play a pivotal role in shaping and supporting the business agility model at Abu Dhabi Police, which has become known internally as 'police agility'.

In a commissioned assessment of the business agility of the Abu Dhabi Police by the current author and colleague consultants in the summer of 2021, part of our findings was that there are many strengths in terms of the agility of the Abu Dhabi Police demonstrated during the COVID-19

Crisis. These include ongoing work and process on future foresight, widespread existence and evidence of innovation, clear leadership and the strength of the Abu Dhabi Police's Business Continuity system. There was evidence of agile practices across all Sectors and Directorates. There was also substantive evidence of an intrinsic implicit understanding of the broad need for, and concept of, agility across the teams interviewed. In addition, there were numerous impressive examples of specific agile responses to changing needs and circumstances, including changes to policies, processes, use of resources and deployment. This included collaborative planning and working with other key stakeholders in Federal and Abu Dhabi government, as well as the wider society. As just one example, the speed and extent of moving staff to remote working were impressive.

In 2021, in its new strategic plan 2021–2025, the police adopted 'institutional flexibility' as one of its strategic objectives as a priority for corporate leadership. Since the COVID-19 pandemic, its approach to business agility has expanded from 'risk management, crisis management and business continuity assurance only' to include all administrative, technical and logistical police operations. As a result of these efforts, Abu Dhabi Police GHQ has received the highest possible rating for institutional flexibility, 3-Star, by the International Consortium of Organisational Resilience (ICOR), and Business Agility Award — Diamond level, by Harvard Business Council International (HBC), and is the first police authority in the world to receive this classification. See Figure 5.2.

The UAE and Abu Dhabi Emirate Governments have also long placed emphasis on future foresight for government entities. Subsequent to the start of the COVID pandemic, attention has also been given to entities' pre-emptiveness in addressing emerging threats. During the 2020 COVID-19 Crisis, Abu Dhabi Police leaders accordingly moved the concept and culture of policing agility from crisis management, security events, risk management and business continuity to the ones of future foresight, sensing developments, capturing opportunities, adapting quickly to the variables, needs and requirements of stakeholders, promoting institutional learning and providing continuous support for development processes.

The Abu Dhabi Police also established a specialised organisational unit for Crisis and Disaster Management with the aim of dealing with

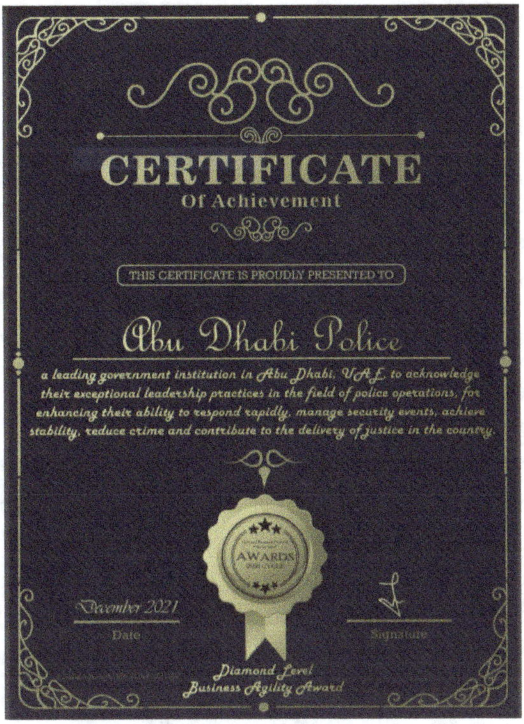

Figure 5.2. The Abu Dhabi Police Business Agility Award — Diamond Level from the Harvard Business Council International

any disturbance, crisis or disaster effectively and efficiently, and working to prevent them through the implementation of the security event management system. They have implemented a business continuity system compatible with ISO 22301 and established an integrated Crises and Disasters database and are working to reduce their effects when they occur and speed recovery therefrom.

At the operational level, the Abu Dhabi Police comply with the guidance in the ISO 31000 risk management international standard, as well as the Business Continuity Management standard, ISO 22301, and the Procedure Guide for Preparedness and Readiness. Accordingly, all police sectors and departments identify key functions and operations, and identify the resources and staff needed to keep the Abu Dhabi Police working flexibly and smoothly during disruptions, crises and disasters.

The Crisis and Disaster Department ensures that these security plans are integrated into the various police departments and measures their ability to deal with any anticipated or unanticipated scenarios that may occur. This has proved effective in dealing with the COVID-19 Crisis.

Their two guides of risk management and impact analysis on vital processes to be restored within seven days include 144 operations, risk assessment for each process, and analysis of process recovery requirements including human resources, worksites, partner technology, suppliers, equipment and documents.

Abu Dhabi is considered the world's leader in the cities security index 2017–2019 according to the standards of private security companies and risk monitoring. In order to increase readiness, it considers potential risks and measures the extent of its success in dealing with them. Mock drills are utilised to measure the extent of success in dealing with risks, and the success rate of risk management plans response has always been 100%.

The risks were reassessed during the COVID-19 Pandemic, particularly the impact of that pandemic on the health and safety of workers and customers, and six high probability and impact risks were identified. These included electronic crimes as the pandemic changed traditional retail purchase behaviour towards electronic, resulting in a heightened risk of criminal activity and electronic hacking. This prompted the creation of new prevention measures, in addition to measures related to infection-associated health hazards, such as working remotely, presenting detainees to the prosecution remotely, and providing services electronically.

Based on its successful experience during the COVID-19 Crisis, the Abu Dhabi Police GHQ launched its new strategic plan for 2021–2025 in mid-2021, emphasising the need to enhance business agility through 'Future Foresight', 'Proactive Services' and 'Innovative Services' for the first time to enable it to deal with unforeseen events. The new Abu Dhabi Police message states the following:

> *'We are working to maintain a sense of security and safety in the Emirate of Abu Dhabi, to achieve police institutional leadership that foresees the future with proactive innovative services that enhance the quality of community life in order to achieve its vision of being the best police force in the world.'*

Blue Bella Limited, London

Established in 2005, BLUEBELLA is a fashion lingerie brand based in London, England, with about 40 employees and, in 2021, was ranked number two on the Top Two Hundred Female-Powered Businesses in the UK in a report by J.P. Morgan. Its business is split between e-commerce sales and wholesale channels. It currently has seven country-facing websites, covering the US, the UK, Australia, France, Germany, Italy, and the rest of Europe. Wholesaling is global, but most limited in Asia and the Middle East, and largest in Europe, the US and Australia.

BLUEBELLA has a core range but is constantly bringing forward new products. Lingerie typically suffers from the longest production times in fashion, due to its many components, and this, together with the associated need for an extensive size range (up to 40 sizes for bras), means that it is usually seen as one of the most complex areas in fashion. There are some European suppliers, but most products are produced in third-party factories in China, implying typical one month shipping times to BLUEBELLA's third-party logistics partner, Torque's, warehouse in Leeds, UK, through which most products are routed.

As a small entrepreneurial business at the difficult end of the fast-moving retail fashion industry, BLUEBELLA both lacks extensive formalised systems for risk management and business continuity and possesses a culture, agility and pre-emptiveness that held it in good stead when faced with the emerging COVID-19 Crisis. Its philosophy was speed, quick decisions and taking action. Accordingly, it monitored the global situation, saw what was happening in Italy, and mobilised fast, two to three weeks ahead of the UK's home working directive in March 2020. The immediate mobilisation saw the identification of what would be needed for the team to work remotely including the provision of laptops.

At this point, BLUEBELLA's focus on business continuity was established emphasising maintaining cash flow and protecting the brand. It was decided to be 'first in the queue' for the newly announced UK Government's Coronavirus Business Interruption Loan Scheme (CBILS) under which a term loan of up to five million pounds was available to SME businesses across the UK that were losing revenue and seeing their cash flow disrupted, as a result of the COVID-19 outbreak. Accordingly, preparation work began immediately.

Initially, the company's three main concerns were the following:

1. A concern that presold stock for wholesale partners would be refused.
2. Their warehouse would need to shut down due to staff sickness, impacting e-commerce and cash flow.
3. Lack of clarity on how global demand would behave.

Reflecting their entrepreneurship, immediately, before mid-March 2020, the MD and Finance Director worked through varied possible scenarios, considered their budget and finance model and did 'What Ifs'. A principle of 'only spending to get cash' was established, and a freeze on hires, a hold on technology projects and reduced PR costs were implemented. A key consideration was the extent of their digital marketing spend, which is one of the company's biggest costs. As a precaution, the company monitored key e-commerce KPIs on a daily basis with a view to adjusting marketing spending in line with any decrease in conversion rate to ensure no wasted cost.

The first concern identified above, that presold stock for wholesale partners might be refused by them, reflecting global demand uncertainty and leading to an excess of stock holding, was major. Such an excess of stock could then lead to major discounting, damaging the brand. The company decided to take a proactive, rather than a reactive, approach to managing this risk. To do this, it took the lead on the control of stock and worked collaboratively and communicated openly, both with its suppliers and its wholesale customers. Work with suppliers focused, where possible, on collaboratively reducing or rescheduling supply. Instead of waiting nervously for the risk of them cancelling out, wholesale customers were then offered the opportunity to reduce their orders to protect their business and the BLUEBELLA brand. Because BLUEBELLA had moved very fast, this was typically ahead of them having identified appropriate action and this pre-emptiveness was welcomed.

BLUEBELLA has also during COVID worked to build in bigger buffer times in its logistics and, during 2021, has greatly increased its use of airfreight. Its focus is on real-time management of both its supply chain and distribution network.

During the COVID-19 Crisis, many employees in organisations globally were involved in remote homeworking, which indirectly resulted in the lack of understanding of what was happening in their business, leading to uncertainty, disorientation, concern and lack of effective team working. At BLUEBELLA, the dangers of disorientation were identified at the start and full transparency, and constant communication was instigated. Weekly updates to the team and regular 'everybody' meetings and socials took place online and a well-being course was run. A difficult decision was also taken to temporarily postpone payment of the previous year's bonus, to protect cash flow, but this received full staff understanding.

Reflecting on the brand philosophy and ethical policies, and similarly supporting its 650,000 followers on Instagram, the company considered what should be their role as a business during COVID-19 isolation. They focused on communication and to 'make people smile', to do a little good. Examples were donating the profit from their sale of facemasks to a domestic violence charity (as domestic violence had increased dramatically during the pandemic), the running of the world's largest fashion show online, and the opportunity every Thursday to nominate a National Health Service worker for free lingerie.

For BLUEBELLA, being based in the UK, the COVID-19 pandemic came among the significant disruption of Brexit. Alongside managing the COVID impact, the company brought forward production to deliver stock to EU partners ahead of the UK's departure from the EU. Subsequently, it has set up an EU entity and is establishing a bonded warehouse.

BLUEBELLA's success through the COVID-19 Crisis is evidenced in varied ways. In 2021, for the third time, it won the prestigious UK Drapers Award for the Lingerie Brand of the Year. See Figure 5.3. More importantly perhaps, following 40% year on year growth in turnover in 2019, it managed to maintain growth at 20% in 2020 as it deliberately held back production at the start of the pandemic due to concerns about global demand, before returning to around 35% year on year growth in turnover in 2021.

Nottingham City Council

Nottingham is a core city in Nottinghamshire in central England's Midlands region. See Figure 5.4. It is famous for its role in the Robin Hood

Figure 5.3. BLUEBELLA Winning the Prestigious UK Drapers Award for the Lingerie Brand of the Year 2021, for the Third Time

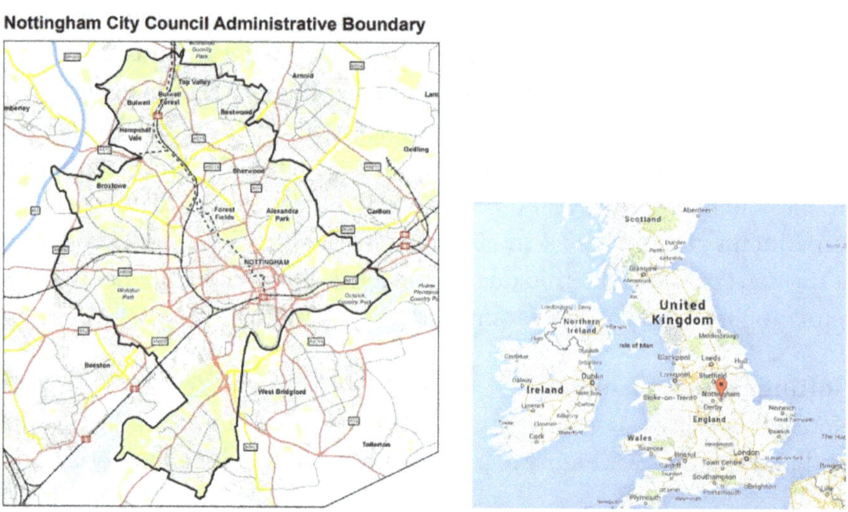

Figure 5.4. Map of Nottingham City Council Area

legend and for the hilltop Nottingham Castle, rebuilt many times since the medieval era, as well as its historical Lace Market area. Nottingham City Council is the council for the unitary authority of Nottingham, meaning that within its boundaries, Nottingham City Council is responsible for all local government functions, which is distinct from the two-tier system of local government in most of England, under which local government functions are divided between county councils (the upper tier) and district or borough councils.

Accordingly, the COVID-19 pandemic provided a major challenge for Nottingham City Council, as it did for local and national governments globally. The Council mobilised early and worked with its partner organisations in the Nottingham and Nottinghamshire Local Resilience Forum to maintain services and prevent, reduce and contain COVID-19 infection. Nottingham City and Nottinghamshire County Councils first produced Local Outbreak Control Plans (LOCPs) in June 2020 as part of a national strategy to reduce infection from COVID-19. In March 2021, local plans were refreshed, incorporating the learnings of the past nine months and planning for the next phase of the response.

With a focus on protecting vulnerable citizens and about 90 distinct services affected by the Nottingham Outbreak Control Plan, each with common and distinct needs, business continuity for Nottingham City Council was a complex and demanding requirement. There were numerous examples of good or outstanding practices, but here we will focus particularly on just one of these. We shall consider Personal Protective Equipment (PPE) supply. As elsewhere, this is an area of significance, with the UK Department of Health's annual accounts reporting that £8.7 billion spent on PPE in 2021 had been written off, and £2.6 billion was spent on kits 'not suitable' for use in the UK's National Health Service in 2021 alone.

Early 2020 saw a rapid demand for Personal Protective Equipment (PPE) across public sector services and strategic partners as a primary response to combat the infection rates and protect vulnerable citizens and key workers from COVID-19. Normal management of PPE was not designed for a significant increase in demand and distribution. Rapidly, Nottingham City Council's stocks were at critical levels, impacted by the UK supply crisis and the panic for items. In addition, the existing physical storage capacity, the locations, and the lack of processes to record distribution complicated the understanding of stock levels and the flow of items. Also, the original arrangements were informal and fragmented across the organisation; one core store used a Day Care centre, where care workers would come, have a coffee, and help themselves to PPE. This was immediately closed due to lockdown restrictions.

Nottingham City Council formed an emergency group to ensure that current PPE stocks owned by the Council were understood, centralised, and used in priority areas. They would meet twice daily by video call to ensure stock levels and to develop a new solution.

The physical centralisation of all major PPE stocks was crucial, with the capacity to deal with a major increase in volumes as demand increased rapidly. Location and layout were critical, and Council's flagship Sports Centre was ideal. The application of lean tools and techniques was used to design the layout and smart processes: visual management tools to ensure new stock was quarantined correctly; spaghetti diagrams to sequence items; and labelled zones for correct storage. Many incoming stock items from the UK relief sources were missing an English language description from the outer packaging, and to open them would break the clinical seal. Thus, quick-thinking staff used the Google Translate app on their mobile telephones to convert the language and clearly mark boxes with colour tags and text, essential for the identification of FFP2 or FFP3 masks.

The other priority was on the distribution of the appropriate PPE to the critical services. A quick development of an ordering web system used an agile methodology; so, a basic functioning request system was live within two weeks. This expanded its functions to quicker authentication, authorisation, and pick-up. Care workers could select items in stock, get management approval, and select a pick-up time slot within a 3-hour window. The care worker would then be issued a QR code to show as authentication at pick-up. A counterintuitive decision was made to provide the live stock levels to care workers at ordering. The risk was panic ordering as items became low, but this actually reduced demand, as care workers only ordered what they needed for their period, thus breaking the 'stockpiling PPE for a month's work' behaviour. Also, links to PPE guidance were built into the ordering solution. This reduced the misunderstanding that workers needed to have the high-level protection PPE, which was at the highest risk and cost.

Rapid development, by a cross-organisational team, was crucial to the new distribution centre and management system. Stock management and distribution are not normal local authority functions. The main ordering and stock management system was developed in-house using existing customer transaction software (Firmstep/Granicus). Assessment of options and quick decisions were supported by lean tools and techniques. These were ideal for this type of situation: data collection, demand analysis, process maps, flow, kanbans and the use of visual management boards. See Figure 5.5.

The distribution centre was able to upscale operations to cover demand from wider strategic partners. Quickly, it became the hub for all PPE requirements, supplying care homes, schools, and other essential workers. Verification routines used Open Data sources (Companies House, Charity Commission, OFSTED and Care Quality Commission) to authenticate partners and ensure the correct distribution. The risk of fraud was significant and credible as other local authorities had seen. The complexity of arrangements could have led to duplication of orders and provide PPE to a non-funded institution. Likewise, just knowing the exact establishment

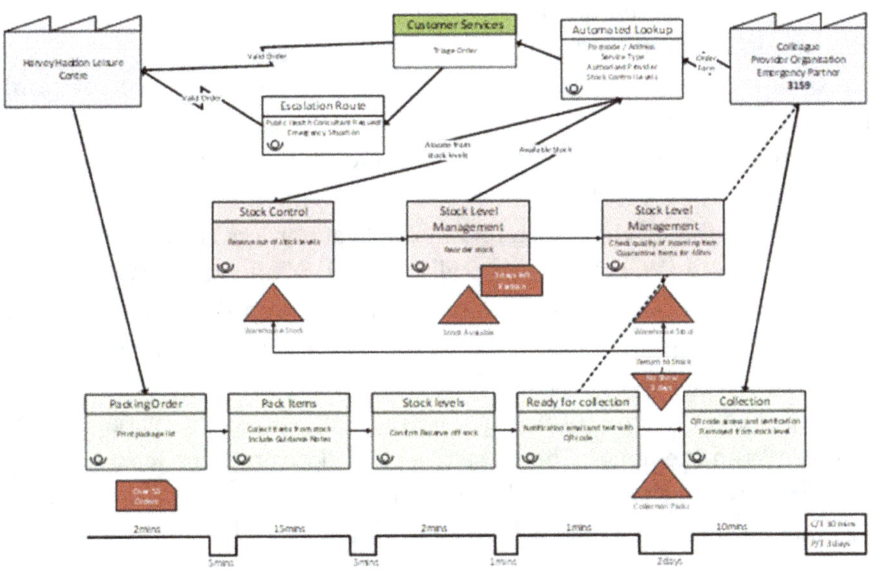

Figure 5.5. Value Stream Map for PPE Stock Management

name, contact details and location was crucial. Previously, establishments' names were not that important but workers and administrators knew these by local and even old names. Routines were adjusted and collection hours were extended to accommodate an increased demand while maintaining social distancing rules.

The monitoring and reporting functions used existing Microsoft products. Visual dashboard provided instant stock levels, orders in progress, and daily burn rates. This allowed for a live proactive/predictive analysis. Although outside factors could disrupt demand quickly, the stock on critical items did not prevent supply to any priority services; and when gaps in supply were forecast, priorities could be quickly re-assessed.

Risk management was normally approached through a project management method, which rated risk by likelihood and impact. PPE distribution used a method based on Failure Mode Effect Analysis (FMEA) that introduced a third factor, detectability. This was used in the distribution flow design and stock management solution. Ultimately, this prevented wrong and faulty PPE from being distributed to care workers. In the emergency unfolding, the supply chain was awash with poor quality PPE. A number of items supplied by the Government sources had no manufacturing quality standards or testing certification and were downgraded or destroyed.

Data standards can be overlooked in the development of a solution. The focus is normally on functionally and technical specifications. Data are often left to the user (client/customer) to input. However, this creates a flaw, as users can, and often, enter details slightly differently, making it difficult to authenticate and results in duplicate orders. The development of semantic web (Web 3.0), specifically open data, allowed the solution to manage/foolproof orders by linking data from a drop-down list. Business and establishment orders can then be verified easier through a loop-back messaging service (SMS/email).

The whole system (ordering, distribution, and stock management) was seen as an exemplar of best practice by the Government Taskforce and partners. It was used to inform the regional PPE management arrangements and was considered a regional distribution centre.

6

Timely Emergence

Introduction

For an organisation or individual, there is a criticality to emerging from a Crisis footing at the right time and in the right way. Too soon, will lead to unnecessary risk and loss. Too late, will miss opportunities. How to emerge also matters greatly, as it sets the level of risk.

Writing in August 2015 on the cover of Deloitte's The Future of Supervision 6, (see Figure 6.1) Charlotte Insinger said the following:

> *After a crisis, you need to get back to normal, and that can be tricky.*

But should we return to 'Normal', as we instinctively usually want to? What is 'Normal' anyway? Is it 'Business as Usual'? 'Normal' working or operations may no longer be appropriate nor 'Normal' thinking. As we know post-COVID-19, the world and circumstances may have changed irretrievably, or indeed, for the better.

Today, we talk glibly about 'The New Normal'. Wikipedia reproduces a definition of this from an article in World Economic Forum as follows[1]:

> *A new normal is a state to which an economy, society, etc. settles following a crisis, when this differs from the situation that prevailed prior to the start of the crisis. The term has been employed in relation to World War I, financial crisis of 2007–2008, September 11 attacks, the aftermath of the 2008–2012 global recession, the COVID-19 pandemic and other events.*

[1] *Source*: Wikipedia 'New normal' accessed on 5th May 2021.

Figure 6.1. The Desire to Return to Normal.
Source: Deloitte 'The Future of Supervision', https://www2.deloitte.com/content/dam/Deloitte/global/Documents/Risk/gx-cm-future-of-supervision.pdf accessed on 5th May 2021.

The phrase is of relatively recent origin, and the concept implies that after a Crisis, we may not return to the same 'Normal' as we had before, pre-Crisis, but to a new version of 'Normal', changed perhaps because of the Crisis. For organisations and their people, this may be a new way of working, such as home working, or a shortened supply chain, or an amalgamation of many such individual changes. Still though, such a 'New Normal' reflects a desire for return to stability, albeit a different one.

But in reality, in a VUCA environment, it's worse than that; stability is not itself normal. So, back in 2020, the current author coined the following phrase:

The New Normal is a Cascade of New Normals.

So, what is 'Emergence' from a Crisis? It is not necessarily a return to how things were pre-Crisis, but it is a return to some sort of new stability that may itself be short lived. It may, indeed, be a fundamentally different concept of stability, such as one that incorporates a new cyclical element or a cascade. 'Emergence' incorporates a redefinition, indeed a reimagining of non-Crisis. However, whatever 'Emergence' is, it is about the Crisis being resolved, completed, finished, ended, and a change of state.

This chapter focuses on determining When and How an organisation should emerge from the Crisis to ensure a successful outcome.

Criticality of Emergence at the Right Time, in the Right Way

As we have discussed above, Emergence from a Crisis is not necessarily the same as 'returning to Normal'. The presumption, implicit or explicit, of returning to 'normal' is, however, a common one. As an illustration, simply Googling *Can't Wait To Get Back To Normal* gave over 2,000,000,000 results. See Figure 6.2.

This was not surprising at what then seemed to be the end of the COVID-19 pandemic in the UK. Looking at some of the various articles identified in the search suggests that many of these articles concern individual citizens' responses to the restrictions on 'normal life' associated with lockdown. Nevertheless, organisations, and individuals within organisations, have a strong desire to return to 'normality' also.

For an organisation, there is criticality in the emergence from the Crisis, not just at the right time but also in the right way. While our human inclination may be a preference for things to revert to how they were, this may not be the best option for the organisation or even perhaps feasible. The need and/or positive opportunity for change may have been there pre-Crisis, appeared during the Crisis, or may be emergent only now.

The need for such change may reflect an ongoing mega trend, such as the rise of technology, the delayed recognition of a latent 'Grey Rhino', such as an ageing population, or the appearance of a disruptive step-change associated with the Crisis, or not. Arguably, perhaps, in the past, we did not change enough.

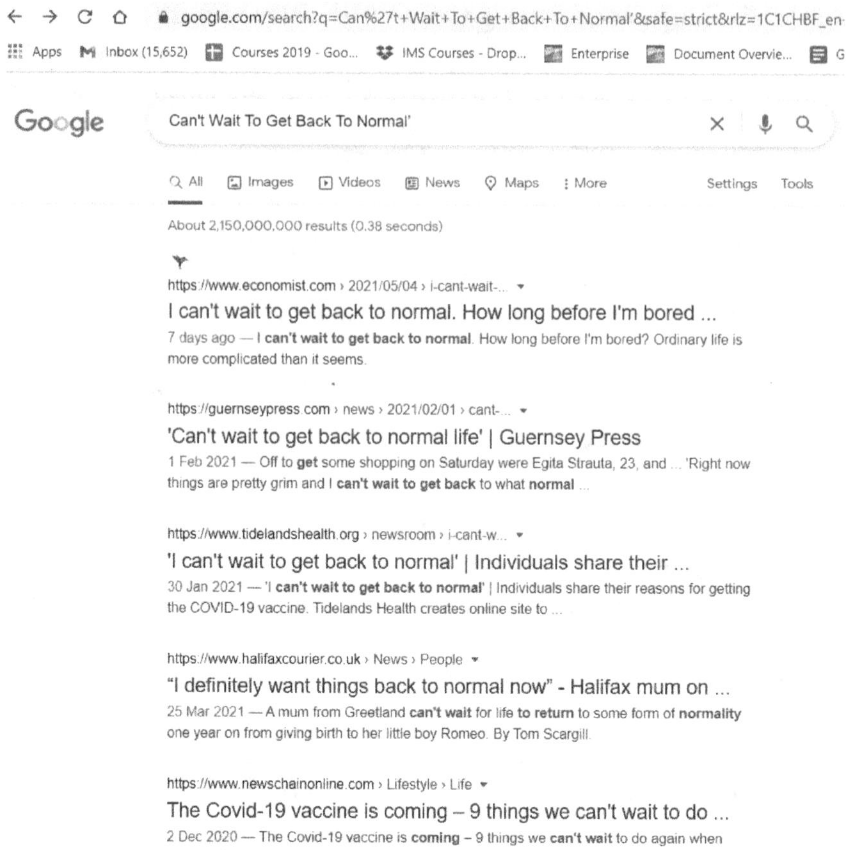

Figure 6.2. Extract from Google for 'Can't Wait To Get Back To Normal' on 11th May 2021

For many, the opportunity is how to emerge stronger from a Crisis. For example, as well as the desire to 'return to normal', many commentators have also seen needs and opportunities for more fundamental change, as the COVID-19 pandemic subsides. To illustrate, for Deloitte, *every looming Crisis is a chance to improve,* while PwC looks to *turn a Crisis into an opportunity.*

Exactly what the required key dimensions of change are today, the transformational requirements of the New Normal and their timetable for implementation, vary with authors. For example, in May 2020, McKinsey argued that to emerge stronger from the COVID-19 Crisis, companies should start reskilling their workforces. Their case was that adapting employees' skills and roles to the post-pandemic ways of working will be crucial to building operating-model resilience.

It is apparent in this discussion that an organisation's timely emergence from a Crisis, at the right time and in the right way, is an important governance and leadership issue. As Willem Stevens writing in Deloitte's 'The Future of Supervision 6' points out, *The real crisis would be non-executive directors who do not see a crisis coming*, but attention to the Crisis **ending** is also crucial.

Emergence from the Crisis requires Leadership, as someone or some group makes the decisions to revert towards 'business as usual' or the 'New Normal'. Decisions have to be made, and steps have to be taken, however tentative, to initiate restoration or the establishment of the new operational model.

A well-thought through approach, therefore, will have good timely information and clearly pre-identified decision makers, decision-making processes and decision criteria, with ongoing review and adjustment. The Leadership aspect remains important because to be successful, emergence and the associated decision-making cannot be a purely rule-based automatic process.

In emerging from a Crisis, it is important to recognise that emergence itself is a process and it is helpful to have an Emergence Checklist for Leaders, in line with broader Crisis Management principles, to assist this. Typical considerations for Leaders during emergence are the following:

1. Seeking from the beginning to continuously understand the situation
2. Clearly taking responsibility
3. Expressing regret and taking action
4. Being proactive, transparent and accountable
5. Proactively avoiding and managing any social media issues
6. Continuously monitoring, planning and communicating
7. Always being prepared
8. Remembering to behave like humans.

Another aspect of how to emerge from Crisis is the extent to which our organisation takes tentative, hesitant small steps or, at the other extreme, bold insightful large ones. Indeed, it can be argued that in all cases, emergence is a process with tentative steps that may need to be halted, reversed, compensated for, or varied depending upon how things unfold. The Path of Emergence is itself emergent as conditions in the ecosystem change and the impact, or otherwise, of the initial tentative steps begins to be realised.

Not all organisations will emerge at once; there is a staggering at the end of the Crisis for organisations, dependent on their circumstances and attitude to risk. An organisation's Path of Emergence is typically conditioned by its organisational history, culture and risk appetite, as well as by the psychological make-up of its Leaders and key stakeholders. But the desire for a 'return to normal' or on occasion perhaps to a new stability, a New Normal, can be very strong.

Just as Knowing the Crisis is Here can be difficult, difficult to be sure of the tipping point given its exponential growth, so too can Knowing the Crisis is Over or Ending be difficult. As was apparent in the COVID-19 Crisis, particularly locally, but also globally, the end of a wave is not necessarily the end of the Crisis. But, nevertheless, responding fast to the Crisis finishing, if it is safe to do so, is desirable for an organisation and will give considerable competitive advantage. Accordingly, neither an entirely Gung Ho nor an entirely conservative approach is likely to be appropriate; Emergence should be specific to the circumstances of the organisation, tentative, subject to change of pace and direction, and not quite full throttle.

Determining When

Since the Emergence is itself a process, an organisation's Path of Emergence can be considered perhaps in general terms as a random walk, with organisational leadership setting and constantly resetting direction, but with stochastically varying interim outcomes, steps and durations. See Figure 6.3.

So, how do we determine when to commence Emergence and when, step by step, to progress it? In some Crises, once Emergence has commenced, unless the timing or conditions of it have been misjudged badly, Emergence itself will be relatively fast. The determinant here is the impact that the Crisis has had on the resources and market conditions

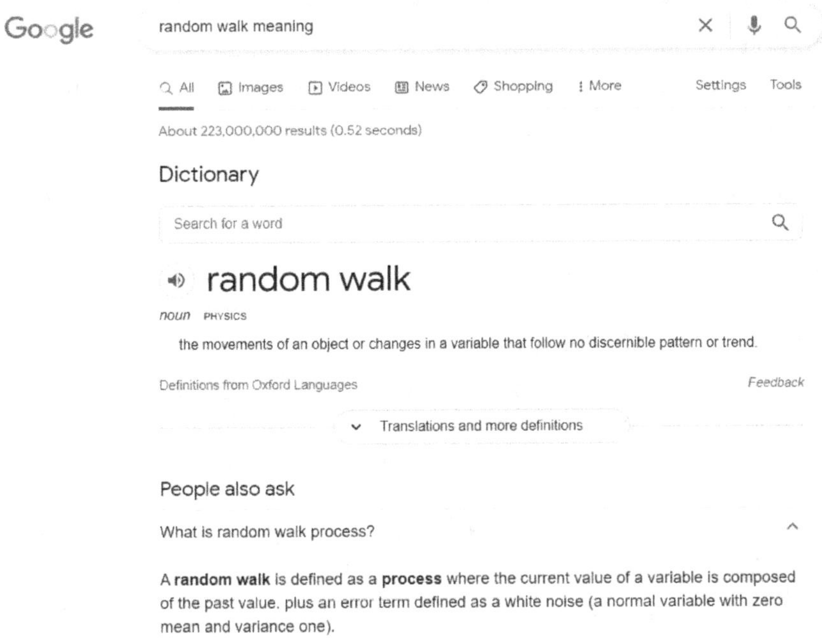

Figure 6.3. Extract from Google for 'Random walk meaning' on 14th May 2021

required for Emergence. For example, has it destroyed or damaged communication, technology or financial resources, or affected markets or supply chains and logistics, needed for Emergence? If not, then the speed of global communication and markets may enable near instantaneous return to normal or new normal.

However, human behaviour, and by implication confidence, will greatly affect the speed of realisation of this; there is a need not just for Normal to be restored but for all, or most, of us to believe that that is the case. This relates back to our discussion of Expectation Influenced Probability in Chapter 1. In reality, there will be a distribution of market behaviour and confidence amongst the population, and of particular relevance will be the organisation's leaders and customer groups.

Conventional organisational risk management leads us to expect that organisations and their leadership teams vary considerably in their propensity to take and accept risk, with a strong correlation within specific sectors. The speed of Emergence is likely to, therefore, reflect this as, indeed, is the likelihood of a 'false start' emergence, with the timings or conditions of Emergence having, initially at least, being judged badly. The higher the appetite for risk, in broad terms, the higher the propensity for earlier Emergence with the greater risk of associated 'false starts'.

Conversely, leaders and organisations that are risk-adverse are likely to be more reticent to return to 'normality' in their operations until the return to Normal, or New Normal, is firmly established, verified and believed to be stable. These may, therefore, lose competitive and other advantages in their hesitancy and returning 'late'.

The difficulty is that in a VUCA environment, such a restoration of Normality or 'New Normality' is inherently deeply uncertain and dynamic, particularly so if, indeed, the New Normal is a Cascade of New Normals, as we proposed above. So, there will be misjudged timing and conditions and 'false starts' emergence. We saw this in the COVID-19 Crisis as successive waves and lockdowns reversed emergence plans in hospitality, travel and traditional retail. But some were perhaps too conservative too, were not ready for reopening on time, and missed opportunities and revenue.

The above argument raises the following three key practical question areas in relation to Emergence:

1. What should be the organisational tests for Emergence?
2. Should the return to Normal working in the organisation not just be based on a time trigger?
3. How should the organisation deal with a potential cascade of New Normals?

Based on its risk appetite, an organisation should establish pre-set criteria for commencing, and for continuing, Emergence. In Chapter 4, we discussed early warnings and leading indicators for the unfolding Global Crisis once it has arrived. Similarly, we can consider early warnings and leading indicators for the end of the Crisis. These should be the basis for organisational decision-making on when it's safe to Emerge.

Clearly, there can be commonality here with the potential for use of the same or similar indicators as we discussed in Chapter 4. As there, the R number could be an important choice and, as there, where we are using a clearly defined leading indicator such as the R number, pre-set warning and/or action levels for that indicator can be established to automate the initiation of an additional review or Emergence action as the Crisis recedes. However, due to the danger of repeating waves of the pandemic, it is likely that this will need to be carefully considered alongside other metrics, the context of the organisation, and its leaders' and stakeholders' opinions based on the best information.

A time trigger for a return to Normal working in an organisation is attractive for its simplicity, but naïve as the length of a Crisis, and the waves of a Crisis, are not standard, predetermined nor easy to accurately forecast.

All of this adds to the need to consider the Path of Emergence for an organisation as a path without a prespecified number of steps, in which following commencement, each subsequent review may progress Emergence further, or halt or backtrack it. Consequentially, its duration is uncertain.

If there is the possibility of a potential cascade of New Normals, the implication is that there should possibly be a Cascading Organisational Emergence Process. What would this look like? This would be a world in which the volatility, uncertainty, complexity and ambiguity we experience at the beginning of a Global Crisis do not resolve themself into a stable recognisable pattern but instead cascades discontinuously from one temporary stability to another, without a clear demonstrable pattern. So, there is no pattern for us to exploit globally nor at the organisational level in regaining control.

Such circumstances used to be seen as exceptional but are intrinsic to the concept of a VUCA environment. In reality, with most Crises, there will be within them extensive continuities of 'Normality' across many dimensions because at the macro level, societies and economies tend to change very slowly. The discontinuities causing a cascade of New Normals, however, may be driven by even bigger things than disruptions, such as the COVID-19 Pandemic, such as the mega trends of climate change and the retooling of the global energy economy.

If the organisation has to deal with a potential cascade of New Normals, a Cascading Emergence Process can be considered, with small tentative emergent steps and frequent review/decision points. However, this is not really then about Emergence from a Crisis, as such, rather the artificial division between Normal, Crisis and New Normal may have become blurred and the Crisis is no more than another Normal. Such a stepping through Normalities is thus regular — a new form of stability.

Determining How

Since we tend to underestimate the chance of a Crisis and the realistic question is not so much if a Crisis will ever occur, but when, arguably then every new Crisis is a chance to improve, just as with a major disaster or Health and Safety incident. For all of these, evaluation of the initiating circumstances, our preparedness and responsiveness are both an opportunity and imperative for change and improvement.

Deloitte presents an argument that while a Crisis can turn existing relations around, usually brings to light new opportunities and allows an organisation to emerge stronger from the Crisis, these opportunities do have to be actively sought out.[2]

The suspension of normal operations during the Crisis provides the opportunity for reflection, reimagining and redesign. Indeed, nothing helps an organisation to gain focus like a Crisis. According to Jacob Middeldorp, *Organisations are usually at their best during crisis situations … Everyone works towards the same goal and all previous conventions seem to disappear.*

We tend to rally around and be mutually supportive during a Crisis too. We have a new sense of purpose, and the solidarity and alertness that come with a Crisis can be a powerful tool which can also be exploited for change.

It follows that Emergence and return to Normal, or New Normal, should incorporate an upgrading of operations and an improved fitness for purpose.

An illustration of this view is contained in Nassim Nicholas Taleb's book *Antifragile: Things that Gain from Disorder*. Taleb argues that organisations should not aim to develop resilience to Crises because being resilient means simply getting back to where they were before. Instead, organisations should strive to be 'antifragile' and come out of the crisis better than when they went in.

---

[2] https://www2.deloitte.com/content/dam/Deloitte/global/Documents/Risk/gx-cm-future-of-supervision.pdf.

PwC argues that those who don't learn from history end up repeating it. For example, in the run-up to the 2008 Global Financial Crisis, the focus was on insulating banks against the impacts of a Crisis rather than identifying and tackling the root causes. They identify five ingredients for an organisation to turn a Crisis into an opportunity and emerge stronger.[3] These are the following:

1. Preparing the organisation's operational teams to be ready for when a Crisis hits, by conducting a readiness assessment, having a Crisis Management Plan, training the people involved in executing the plan and testing the plan.
2. Ensuring that establishing and evaluating the relevant required facts are rigorous, objective and fast, while being aware and owning up to what you don't know.
3. Facilitating the necessary collaboration between the three key groups of internal teams essential to Crisis response:
   - The legal and regulatory teams responsible for understanding the organisation's risk exposures and advising on appropriate responses.
   - The communications and public relations teams responsible for developing and delivering the organisation's internal and external messaging.
   - The operational response teams that establish the facts that the other two groups need to be able to do their jobs, and handle everything else.
4. Communicating appropriately with all the organisation's stakeholders in ways that authentically reflect its brand values rather than only focusing on communicating with particular stakeholder groups.
5. Learning from mistakes and acting on them, including how to respond more effectively in future, identifying what can be learnt from the effectiveness of the Crisis plans, and how can we improve on them in the future. This is a leadership issue, since if the senior leaders are willing to accept fault and learn lessons, then this 'tone from the top'

[3] https://www.pwc.com/gx/en/issues/crisis-solutions/corporate-crisis-into-opportunity.html

shapes behaviours at all levels and employees will feel empowered to learn lessons as well.

Another aspect of how to emerge from a Crisis could be said for organisational leaders, to be with a level of optimism. Perhaps prematurely in hindsight, in Harpers Bazaar in November 2020,[4] four leading businesswomen shared advice on navigating the uncertainty following the COVID-19 pandemic. Rita Clifton, Eva Lindholm, Maryam Meddin and Rupal Patel discussed the complexities of working life in a world transformed by the pandemic. Their advice included the following:

- Step Out Of Your Comfort Zone
  If Covid has taught us one thing, it's the importance of being comfortable with being uncomfortable. In this climate, you can only plan your life or your business in four- or six-week increments, which is really the way most entrepreneurs survive, because you never know the curveballs your investors, suppliers or the economy will throw your way.
  Rupal Patel, former CIA analyst and the founder of Entreprenora
- Learn To Love Your Imposter
  You know that little voice tapping on your shoulder telling you that you can't do something or should step aside for someone who really knows what they're doing? We can all have that feeling, but that's a normal human thing — 70 per cent of people say they experience imposter syndrome ... But there are so many practical things you can do to build your confidence ... Stay curious about what's happening in the world and keep setting yourself stretch-zone targets.
  Rita Clifton, former vice chairman and strategy director at Saatchi & Saatchi and former CEO and chairman at Interbrand
- Become Fluent In The Language Of Business
  The more confident you are, ... the less stress you will feel ... taking control will help you gain confidence ... You'll realise that much of it is just vocabulary: there's no magic, it's just like learning a foreign language. My number one tip is don't quit. You can't win the game if you quit the game.
  Eva Lindholm, head of wealth management, UK and Jersey, at UBS

[4] https://www.harpersbazaar.com/uk/people-parties/bazaar-at-work/a34698993/how-to-emerge-stronger-from-crisis/

- Take Care Of Yourself
  Being able to let go a bit is important ... But above all, find meaning in what you're doing. If you're getting out of bed every morning motivated only by financial reward, life won't be a lot of fun and you'll find you're forever chasing something that's never going to be enough — so make sure you enjoy the journey.
  Maryam Meddin, founder of the Sok

Successful Emergence

What is successful emergence anyway for an organisation? Successful does not necessarily mean without mistakes. Having no mistakes at all on the Path of Emergence is perhaps unlikely, particularly in a VUCA environment. Indeed, any management team is perhaps unlikely to get it all right. What is important, however, is that overall organisational emergence is successful so that minor errors of judgement on the timing or nature of emergence can be overlooked.

What then are the criteria for judging successful emergence from a Crisis? In the Preface of this book, we effectively defined a Crisis as an impending threat to sustainment. We said there that, in reality, all Global Crises are multidimensional, originating perhaps in part of the sustainability space that is specifically economic, societal or environmental, but then being propagated to crisis point by mechanisms that play out across all spheres of sustainability. It follows that, therefore, emergence from a Crisis should be judged by success in restoring the organisation to an appropriate place in 'Normality' or an appropriate 'New Normal' across the multiple dimensions of sustainability. Thus, arguably, to be successful, organisational emergence needs to make sense economically, societally and environmentally.

The organisation's leadership, therefore, needs to have both continuing breadth and depth in terms of clarity of the current and emergent sustainability environment, as well as the current state of the organisation and the corresponding multidimensional criteria for successful emergence. There is emerging literature on this. For example, the Workshop analysis by Ana Caroline Tavares da Silva et al, published in January 2020, considered three scenarios for the COVID-19 pandemic in 2021 and how to plan the future of your company when the quarantine ends.

Leaders' roles are also changed, and frequently augmented, by Crises. As well as being negative changes in human affairs, times of great disagreement, confusion or suffering, and events that lead to unstable and dangerous situations, Crises are intrinsically frequently tipping points reflecting underlying trends and are consequentially calls to action.

Through experiencing such Crises, organisations identify, accept and respond to underlying issues or environmental changes that may necessitate organisational changes to ensure survivability and thriving. As pointed out by Joseph Amankwah-Amoah, Zaheer Khan and Geoffrey Wood writing in the *European Management Journal* in September 2020,

> *... the COVID-19 pandemic has had more immediate effects on the global business ecosystem. Accompanying the COVID-19 pandemic, with more than 14 million cases and over 600,000 fatalities globally affecting countries across Africa, Americas, Eastern Mediterranean, Europe, South-East Asia, and Western, are multiple cases of foreclosures, massive unemployment, car repossessions, and waves of business failures ranging from retailers, airlines, and health, fitness, and well-being centres, among several others. In the UK, for instance, the pandemic has exponentially led to an increase in the number of financially distressed companies. It is estimated that around "half a million firms are at risk of collapse"*
>
> *..... These demonstrate a looming problem facing the industry and public policy and the need for better understanding of the conditions leading to business failure and how best to mitigate them. As recently observed by Walsh (2020, p. nd), "companies large and small are succumbing to the effects of the coronavirus", and 2020 has been projected to "set a record for so-called mega bankruptcies" ... many small and medium enterprises (SMEs) and multinational enterprises (MNEs) teeter on the edge of closure due to the COVID-19 pandemic...*[5]

Thus, during organisational emergence, leaders may need to have a new focus and take on new roles. As an example, McKinsey has identified the following:

> *All the world's a stage, but the COVID-19 pandemic has rewritten the script. Executives are now asked to play different parts.*[6]

[5] https://www.ncbi.nlm.nih.gov/pmc/articles/PMC7474582/.

[6] https://www.mckinsey.com/business-functions/risk-and-resilience/our-insights/covid-19-implications-for-business.

As an example, they state the following:

> *The job of CFO has been transformed by the pandemic, according to the latest McKinsey Global Survey. Crisis management, social and environmental issues, and the accelerated adoption of technology are occupying time previously devoted to strategic leadership and finance capabilities. Between 2016 and 2021, the share of finance leaders who say that they are responsible for their companies' digital activities has more than tripled. Procurement, board engagement, and investor relations are also newly important focuses for CFOs.*

From the above discussion, we can obviously conclude that Global Crises are simultaneously Threats and Opportunities for organisations and that successful Emergence, as well as survival prior to that, is clearly an issue of Leadership. During Emergence from a Global Crisis, not only does an organisation's leadership need to contend with the current and emergent environment, as well as the current state of the organisation, but specifically also the consequences, many unintended, of its own actions taken during the Crisis to protect its immediate and perhaps future survivability.

Many of these decisions concern Human Resources, and the consequences and legacies of these during and subsequent to the organisation's emergence from the Crisis, can be major. For example, during the COVID-19 pandemic, organisations around the world took difficult decisions involving home working, furloughing employees, reducing headcount, renumeration and role definitions. Such decisions were taken both for reasons of business continuity and protection of employees, as well as compliance with government requirements and financial expediency.

The full consequences of these for both the organisations and the employees within the New Normal are only subsequently becoming apparent. An example is the migration of available workers from sectors now regarded as subject to potential further disruption and risk, such as hotels and hospitality, to what is now popularly perceived as more secure employment, such as in social care. Another is the logistics sector, where the emergent shortages of drivers of Heavy Goods Vehicles is now causing a knock-on effect of a shortage of bus drivers, as workers follow the financial incentives to cover the shortages.

This implies two key considerations in relation to organisational emergence from a Global Crisis. First, the organisation's leadership needs to balance the potential impacts of decisions taken during the Crisis on post-Crisis recovery, with the immediate risks and the benefits obtained from those decisions. The assumption that 'if we protect ourselves now, we will be able to quickly rebuild later' is unlikely to be valid after a Global Crisis when competition to rebuild and successfully emerge are simultaneously the priority of all organisations globally.

Secondly, it is important for the organisation's leadership to realise that for this and broader reasons, successful organisational emergence from a Global Crisis is always likely to include some elements of reskilling the workforce. Substituting for lost employees and skills, remote working, migrating processes to automation or a virtual environment are examples of likely changes that will need skill support.

In broader terms, there is also an issue of the alignment of organisational emergence with market emergence from the Global Crisis. With the COVID-19 pandemic, the changes in consumer behaviour created by the Crisis, such as the growth in online retail purchasing, appear to be major and will have a long legacy. Moreover, while 'a return to the high street' commenced early as lockdowns were lifted around the world, the progress, speed and extent of either a full return to previous consumer behaviour, or the establishment of a very different 'New Normal', remain uncertain. The world has changed, but by how much, or for how long, is not yet fully clear. In such circumstances, the level of financial risk associated with organisational emergence in traditional retail is massive. Emergence in that field, therefore, is of needs cautious.

As well as Human Resources and markets, a third structural consideration concerning organisational emergence is supply chains. The COVID-19 pandemic has distorted supply chains enormously. Early in the pandemic, there was interesting evidence of organisational agility as countries globally tried, with success, to source Personal Protective Equipment and necessary healthcare technology locally. At the time, this appeared to represent a temporary move from an emphasis on the lowest price efficiency of supply, to supply availability and reliability.

As the pandemic progressed, further apparently temporary disruptions to supply chains became apparent as suppliers and logistics were disrupted or shut down temporarily due to government requirements, infection and their own supply chain issues. Ships and containers were in the wrong places, backlogs became greater, some suppliers ceased trading and there were problems sourcing lorry drivers and much else.

This contagion effect, typical of such systemic risks as we see in Global Crises, has reinforced recognition of the already clearly apparent fragility of global supply chains based primarily on the lowest cost. Extended supply chains represent an inherent weakness for an organisation as they involve multiple organisations with diverse ownerships, management, geographies and political systems, all of which include the risk of disruption. The more extended the supply chain, in general, the weaker its integrity and the higher the risk of disruption, especially when up against substantive systemic risks. As with markets, it is still early to be sure whether the post-Covid 'Normal' will be the same as the 'Old Normal' in this regard, or whether this risk will be hedged by some increase in local supply.

Whatever the answer to this, for many organisations, the at least temporary legacy of the COVID pandemic is a residual of somewhat haphazard supply, hence problematic operations and lack of clarity in the most appropriate speed, format and extent of Emergence.

7

After the Crisis

Introduction

The organisation will, in general, wish to schedule its emergence from the Crisis to take the best advantage of a return to 'Normal' or a clearly defined stable 'New Normal'.

How do we know when a Global Crisis is really over, at least just from the perspective of our organisation? What signifies its end and how do we gain confidence that now life for our organisation can potentially return to the 'Normal' or a clearly defined stable 'New Normal'?

The end of global, rather than just organisational, emergence from the Crisis, the start of the immediate post-Crisis period, is both difficult to define in theory and difficult to spot in practice since its identity is largely defined by the psychology of the observers, in this case, the organisation's leaders, customers and other stakeholders.

In general, this recognition and acceptance of the world's post-Crisis status by an organisation is likely to be tentative and gradual because the legacy of the Crisis and difficult times is still apparent, and because emergence and recovery from the Crisis may reveal new disruptive challenges. At the same time, 'wishful thinking' can lead optimistic commentators to identify it too early. All these aspects were apparent in the global COVID-19 Pandemic.

So, when is it all over? For an organisation, the answer has to be when we believe securely that it is. The organisation may just wait for this secure belief to emerge in its Board, leaders or key stakeholders. It may instead be directly guided by government or industry bodies, or global commentators, or it may establish *a priori* its own tests and conditions for the end of the Crisis.

What the tests and conditions are will vary with organisation, its operations, risk appetite, and the levels of uncertainty, complexity and volatility. For the organisation to treat the Global Crisis as over, the common ingredients are likely to be some level of stability in markets, supply, internal labour and operations.

This chapter is concerned with the immediate post-Crisis period, ascertaining we are in it, and planning and deploying recovery. Furthermore, it considers the need to learn lessons and implement that learning, since all too often in the past this has not been done adequately. Finally, it deals very sensibly with preparing for the next Crisis.

Being Sure It Is Over

As we said above, you can't be. But an organisation can, at least, plan and replan based on close monitoring and diagnosis; iterative, gradual and tentative steps; and evaluation, consensus and risk assessment. Global KPIs can provide appropriate indicators too that the Crisis is over.

However, what exactly do we mean by 'the Global Crisis is over' anyway, even just from the perspective of our organisation? You may recall that in Chapter 1, we pointed out that we mislabel Global Crises. We asked there whether a Financial Crisis is purely Financial? And we decided surely not, since its initiation, propagation and consequences all have societal elements other than just economic ones. Similarly, we argued that perhaps the Coronavirus Crisis is not entirely well named, as it has major economic implications and the main determining element in its propagation is not the natural spread of the disease but instead how responding human behaviour affects that and impacts personal, organisational, societal and economic survival.

In reality, all Global Crises are multidimensional, originating perhaps in part of the sustainability space that is specifically economic, societal or environmental, but then being propagated to crisis point by mechanisms that play out across all the three spheres of sustainability. So, what does the Global Crisis being over mean for our organisation? What are the tests and conditions?

We said above that the common ingredients are likely to be some perceived level of stability in our organisation's markets, supply, internal labour and operations. But there remain questions of 'Where?' and 'What?'.

For example, from an organisation's perspective, does a global pandemic have to be ended globally for the Global Crisis to be seen as over or only in specific immediately obviously relevant domains corresponding to the organisation's operations, markets and supply chain? Obviously, with the super interconnectivity of the global economy and society, anything short of globally may not be enough and local occurrences may still recur despite the apparent temporary resolution. And, as many sources point out, e.g., McKinsey (Sarun Charumilind, Matt Craven, Jessica Lamb, Adam Sabow, Shubham Singhal, and Matt Wilson) in August 2021,[1] at a given time, different countries have varying prospects for reaching the end of a pandemic.

The 'What?' raises two further related questions: Stability on What Metrics? and Stability on What Dimensions? The first question would be a relatively easy one provided that attention was restricted to potential metrics based on the Crisis's 'label': a pandemic, a Financial Crisis or whatever. But, as we argue above, restricting it to this one dimension is naive. The impact of a Global Crisis on an organisation is clearly multidimensional, taking place through complex interrelationships and interactions. The COVID-19 Pandemic has impacted organisations' human resources, supply chains, operations and markets. Many of these are still temporarily or permanently disrupted and potentially unstable, so it would be naïve and inherently dangerous for an organisation to treat the Global Crisis it caused as over when the World Health Organisation reduces its status as a pandemic to the status of a localised epidemic.

Who Decides? The Role of the Board in Crises

The strategic importance of the 'Deciding it's over' decision implies that it is likely to be taken by the Board of the organisation, typically on the recommendation of, or with the support of, the organisation's executive

[1] https://www.mckinsey.com/industries/healthcare-systems-and-services/our-insights/when-will-the-covid-19-pandemic-end

team. This, in itself, raises potential issues, since Boards are not necessarily adequately competent, skilled or informed for such decision-making.

This is evidenced, for example, by the 2011 'Roads to Ruin' study report from the Cass Business School which identified seven broad residual risk categories from the study of crises affecting 21 organisations. These were the following:

1. Board skill and non-executive director control
2. Limitations in skills and competence to monitor and control the organisation
3. Board risk blindness
   - Failure to recognise and engage with risks to the same degree that they engage with reward and opportunity
3. Inadequate leadership on ethos and culture
4. Defective internal communication
   - Important information not reaching appropriate staff
5. Organisational complexity and change
   - Includes risks from acquisitions
6. Incentives
   - Includes effects on behaviour that result from both explicit and implicit incentives
7. Risk 'glass ceiling'
   - Inability of risk management and internal audit teams to report to, and discuss risks with, the top management team

The report also identified problems in relation to 'groupthink' and that there were more issues with 'soft skills' than with technical know-how. In addition to these Board issues, Boards may not adequately challenge and evaluate proposals from executive management.

Arguably, when a Crisis emerges, regardless of its origin, boards come under heightened scrutiny and pressure from external sources. They need to make quick decisions, take decisive action, and communicate clearly and regularly with stakeholders and the C-suite.

In 2014, Davia Temin argued that as Crisis has become a new global norm, the board's responsibility in Crisis was changing rapidly and

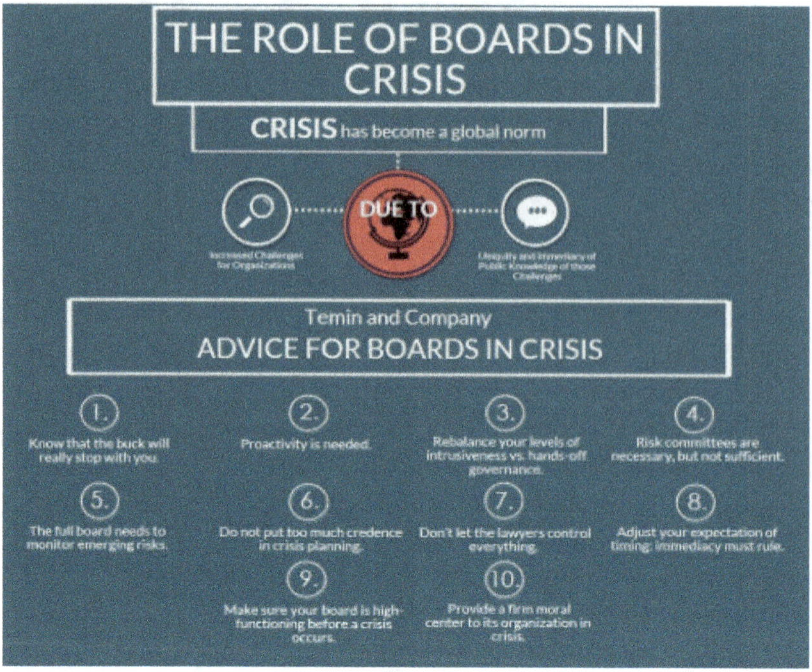

Figure 7.1. The Role of Boards in Crisis

Source: Davia Temin October 8, 2014, Forbes 'The Role Of Boards In Crisis: 10 Steps For Directors Before, During And After Crisis', https://www.forbes.com/sites/daviatemin/2014/10/08/the-role-of-boards-in-crisis-10-steps-for-directors-before-during-and-after-crisis/?sh=6370a4832ba4 accessed on 27th October 2021.

increasing. In her view, the public, shareholders, and media are holding boards responsible for corporate missteps as never before, and, therefore, the role of governance after, as well as leading up to and during, the Crisis was transforming. On this basis, she provided 10 considerations for a Board to do in order to prepare for, possibly prevent, respond to, and recover from the inevitable Crises that will affect their organisations. See Figure 7.1.

More recently, in February 2021, McKinsey hosted a podcast in which three Board Directors discussed the role boards were playing in guiding their companies toward recovery from the COVID-19 Crisis.[2]

In starting the podcast, Celia Huber, McKinsey senior partner, comments that

[2] https://www.mckinsey.com/business-functions/strategy-and-corporate-finance/our-insights/the-boards-role-during-crisis-and-beyond.

After the financial crisis, we saw a trend toward more independent boards that brought their own perspectives as regulation and scrutiny increased. Today, boards are going beyond their core responsibility for oversight of corporate financials and staying on top of things like technological shifts and the company's impact on broader society. Even before the pandemic, we saw boards increasingly dealing with how to preserve corporate resilience, deal with activist investors, monitor corporate culture, and make the right decisions on risks around cybersecurity and other issues. So, the pressure on boards to be fully engaged and act as catalysts for change is coming from many directions now.

She goes on to identify hallmarks of successful Boards in this context as a deep understanding of their industry and key uncertainties, thinking about strategy as part of every board meeting rather than annually or every three years, sharing feedback, strengthening team dynamics, and interacting with management.

Margaret Mulligan then comments that the same factors distinguish a great board in crisis as in normal times, and first and foremost this is understanding and respecting the difference between the board's and management's roles.

Peter Bisson then goes on to say that apart from the 'maybe 10 to 15% of companies for which this crisis is an existential threat', the pandemic does not change most of the priorities. He adds the following:

The test for the board is, can you keep your eye on the key strategic decisions or transformation programs you are pursuing, recognising that the management team might be reaching the saturation point in what it can manage? The board needs to help the management team get done the additional work that comes with a crisis.

In relation to the Board, Margaret Mulligan adds the following:

While the agenda topics have not changed much, the frequency of meetings has, simply because management has to make many tactical decisions and conduct business differently. I do expect there could be some refocusing of agenda items once we all take a breath because we will revisit strategies and enterprise risks. The black swan scenario that we all model — we are living it. I hope there will be a lot of solemn learning from that.

They also discuss the increased speed of decision-making in the Crisis by both management and Boards, and Nora Aufreiter comments that both management and boards have been surprised at how quickly they can take decisions when necessary.

Peter Bisson points out that the chair or lead director has an important role to play in the relationship between the Board and management, in a sense, to police the boundary. He says that while executional decisions are usually left to management, if they carry a reputational dimension, then the management team tends to bring it to the board. However, you do not want the board trying to run the company operationally.

More recently still, in its October 2021 issue, the 'Financier Worldwide' discussed the unique role of boards in crisis management and response. It reports that according to the National Association of Corporate Directors, almost 50% of board members feel that their focus on known risks was a barrier to preparing for threats that may be hard or impossible to predict. Less than 20% felt confident that management could handle these unforeseen risks. Accordingly, there is a need to improve crisis management planning by focusing on frameworks which allow decisions to be approved, implemented and communicated quickly and effectively. Specifically, this article advocates that:

> *Rather than simply rubber-stamping management proposals, a board should draw on its wealth of experience and expertise to offer viable options and provide insights that management may have overlooked.*

The article quotes Harlan Loeb, executive vice president at Argyle Communications, as saying that

> *Ironically boards are thrust into crisis mode themselves when emergencies erupt because they are often ill-equipped and ill-prepared or simply do not have the time to meet the oversight obligations required to prepare for and navigate corporate crises.*
>
> *This is especially troubling since governance oversight organisations have concluded emphatically that crisis and reputation risk oversight is the exclusive province of the board.*

He adds:

> *Too often, boards comprise well-compensated and well-intentioned directors who are too ill-equipped and time-starved to play a meaningful oversight role on crisis and reputation risk governance.*

In this context, a recent PwC survey found that only 37% of respondents described their board's crisis expertise as good or excellent, 57% said they thought the board understood their own company's Crisis Plan very or somewhat well, and executives assessed the board's knowledge of crisis management as the lowest of 10 areas considered.

During a Crisis, the board should play a supportive role, supplementing the work of executive management. The decision-making process should be collaborative, with constant communication between the chief executive and the board. The chief executive should keep the board informed as events unfold and also engage the board in evaluating alternative courses of action, utilising the board's collective experience.

After the Crisis, the board should quickly conduct a Crisis Post-Mortem to analyse the details of how well it and the organisation coped with and managed the Crisis, and the lessons to be learnt. Were we ready? What was the impact? What actions were taken to mitigate and resolve it? How appropriately and how timely? What did we not do so well? What should be done to ensure we can prevent this from happening again? This post-mortem should be a blameless process, an opportunity to learn about and improve on organisational response and processes.

In the immediate post-crisis period, it is also essential that boards ensure momentum is maintained throughout recovery, reimagining and transformation, and that they keep a keen eye on emergent further risks, consequential on the crisis or otherwise.

Recovering

Typically, the organisation is likely to have deployed emergency and Business Continuity arrangements and processes to keep it operational through the Crisis. As well as traditional business continuity management systems, during the COVID-19 Crisis, these have included home working, virtual meetings and furloughing. After emerging from the Crisis, as well as learning for the future, starting sensibly with a post-mortem, the organisation needs to plan and deploy its recovery.

Business continuity kept the organisation going but did not provide permanent 'fixes' to the organisation's operations for the return to Normal or the demands of the New Normal. Such 'fixes' should not be seen in isolation from each other but as a holistic whole. The planning for these now needs to be fine-tuned and deployed. To do this, there is an intrinsic need to look at all aspects of the organisation in a structured way, to avoid omissions and unintended consequences of piecemeal change.

A good basis for this can be the application of one of the established holistic organisational management frameworks, such as the international quality management system standard ISO 9001, organisational excellence models, such as the EFQM or Malcolm Baldrige National Quality Award Model, the McKinsey 7S Model or the Deloitte's Layer Model.

Generally, the so-called Excellence Models represent more extensive and inclusive frameworks for organisations than does the international quality management standard, ISO 9001, and related international standards. Of these, there are three models which have a particular level of global recognition: the European Foundation for Quality Management Excellence (EFQM) Model based in Europe, the Malcolm Baldrige National Quality Award Model based in the US, and the Deming Prize Model of Japan. Each of these models, and the various alternatives and hybrids around the World, attempts to capture the essence of the organisation in a coherent assessment framework based on clearly defined criteria covering the organisations' approaches, their deployment, and their assessment and refinement, as well as the adequacy of the results so achieved.

The EFQM Excellence Model is typical and may be used as an illustration. See Figure 7.2. Owned by the European Foundation for Quality Management based in Brussels, and with partner organisations across Europe and further afield, this structure is based on three sets of questions:

'Why' does this organisation exist? What purpose does it fulfil? Why this particular Strategy? (DIRECTION)

'How' does it intend to deliver on its Purpose and its Strategy? (EXECUTION)

Figure 7.2. The EFQM Excellence Model

Source: https://efqm.org/efqm-model.

'What' has it actually achieved to date? 'What' does it intend to achieve tomorrow? (RESULTS)

Similar to the models of excellence, the international quality management system standard ISO 9001, and the analogous international management system standards, such as those for environmental management and occupational health and safety management, ISO 14001 and ISO 45001, incorporate consideration of the organisation's learning and improvement loops. They also incorporate attention to organisational self-audit by independent personnel, leading to management review and

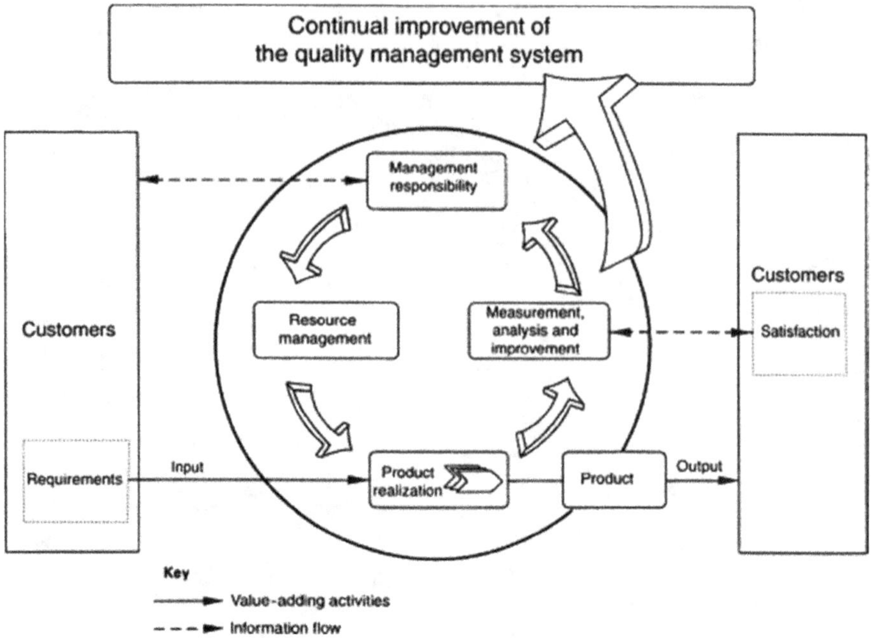

Figure 7.3. The ISO 9001 Process Model

Source: Based on ISO 9001 (2008).

action. It could be argued, however, that in these standards, more emphasis is placed on rule-based compliance so that potentially they are more fragile as organisational models, although this is to some extent mitigated by the extent of interpretation of rules possible. See Figure 7.3.

Like the above models, the McKinsey 7 S Model has reached the Business Schools and, although it perhaps does not provide a coherent holistic theory for the organisation, it does provide insight into linkages sufficient to assist the organisation to improve performance, examine the likely effects of possible changes, align departments and processes during a merger or acquisition, and determine how best to implement a proposed strategy.

The model was developed by Robert H. Waterman Junior and Tom Peters, and is based on a theory that recognises that for an organisation to perform well, the seven named elements need to be aligned and mutually reinforcing. See Figure 7.4.

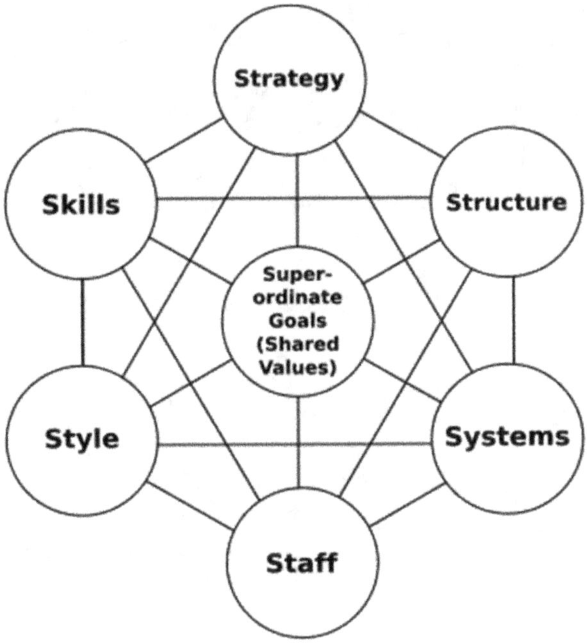

Figure 7.4. The 7 S Model

Source: Peters (2011).

Deloitte's Layer Model in Figure 7.5 is to an extent similar, in that it provides a unified representation of the organisation, to assist selection of strategic choices. The use of this model, in particular, can be very beneficial to allow us to look at all aspects of the organisation in a structured way, to avoid omissions and unintended consequences of piecemeal change, so as to take a holistic approach to evaluate the post-Crisis situation and planning and deploying the organisation's Recovery by focusing on a Target Operating Model.

Having looked at all aspects of the organisation in a structured way by utilising one of these models, there is a need to access the market, operations and supply chain; compare our operations with the old assumptions; scan the horizon; look at trends and potential black swans and grey rhinoceroses; reimagine the possibilities; and reach and implement decisions.

In doing this, the organisation's leadership needs to first recognise its place on the Kubler-Ross Change Curve, or Bereavement Curve (Figure 7.6).

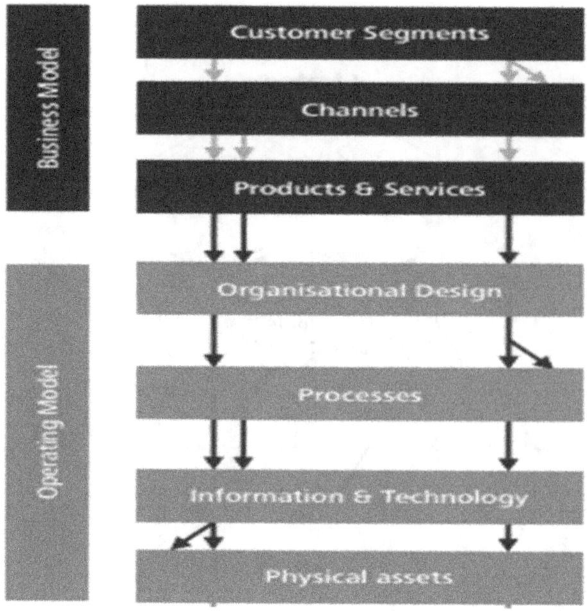

Figure 7.5. Deloitte's Layer Model

This is important because organisations and their leadership can be in shock, denial, anger or depression about the Crisis and consequential change, and there is a need to be conscious of this in order to make sound decisions, especially for recovery.

The Recovery strategy is also likely to be agile or emergent, risk-based and designed to be stakeholder inclusive, taking the people with you.

Learning the Lessons

There are lessons to be learnt from all Crises, but we do not always learn them, at least not fully nor adequately, nor do we necessarily implement what we have learnt. It is a reasonable criticism of responses to recent Global Crises that this is particularly true, at all levels: globally, nationally, and organisationally. For example, following the Financial Crisis while some new safeguards were put in place for banking, especially nationally, these were very much limited. We could, and should, have done more.

Following a Crisis, it is easy to be complacent going forward, since you survived. It is a question of Outcome Bias. In general, learning the lessons,

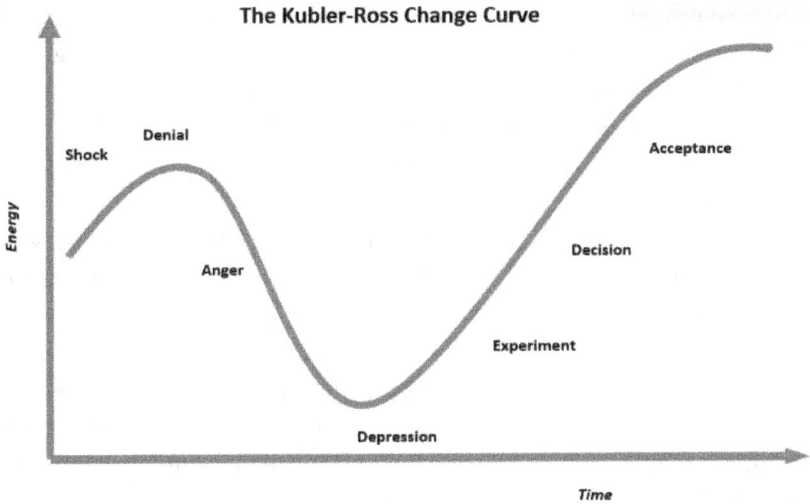

Figure 7.6. The Kubler-Ross Change Curve
Source: Umar Tahir, December 10, 2019, Kubler-Ross Change Curve Model, Change Management Insight, http://changemanagementinsight.com/kubler-ross-change-curve-model/ accessed on 2nd November 2021.

short and long terms, big and small is a crucial aspect of Recovery after the Crisis and preparation for the next one. In a VUCA environment, such as the global environment today, it is even more crucial.

Two key quotations in this regard are

> *Good judgement comes from experience and experience comes from bad judgement.*
>
> Attributed in various phrasing to Mark Twain (Samuel Langhorne Clemens), Dr Kerr L White, Will Rogers, Rita Mae Brown, Bob Packwood, General Omar Bradley, Jim Horning and others.

> *All men make mistakes, but only wise men learn from their mistakes.*
>
> Winston Churchill

Accordingly, learning the lessons following a Crisis, short term for Recovery, and long term as preparation for future Crises, requires careful consideration and planning. After having successfully mobilised and stabilised for Recovery, there is still a need to strategise for the long term.

A first step is to revisit your organisation's crisis response, identifying lessons learned and opportunities for improvement. The following step is to invest in strengthening the organisation's response capabilities, so that they are prepared for future eventualities. After a Crisis, the most successful organisations are typically those that invest in learning lessons, implementing changes, and leveraging opportunities.

PwC's Global Crisis Survey 2021[3] aims to examine the worldwide business community's response to the unprecedented social, economic and geopolitical disruption of the COVID-19 pandemic. Between 20 August 2020 and 25 January 2021, organisations from 73 countries and 29 industries shared their observations. In addition to asking 'How did organisations react to the immediate threats?', the survey gives insight into how businesses are integrating what they have learned into strategies for long-term resilience.

The survey includes responses from 2,814 global business leaders on the impact of the COVID-19 Pandemic on their organisations. More than 70% of respondents said their business was negatively impacted by the Crisis, while interestingly 20% said the crisis had a positive impact and that they were in a better position today than before the pandemic. The top three areas for improvement in organisations that conducted an after-action review were improving Crisis Management, Business Continuity Management and Enterprise Risk Management.

The survey suggests recognition of three main lessons to be learnt. First, the need to better planning and preparation for future Crises. It is recognised that organisations with a strategic crisis response plan can mobilise more swiftly, stabilise business operations and respond effectively to the shockwaves of disruption. In this regard, 95% of business leaders reported that they believed their current crisis management capabilities need improvement.

It is noteworthy that in 2019, 95% of respondents to the first PwC Global Crisis Survey said they expected a crisis to hit within the next two years, although there was no perception that this would be a pandemic. However, when the COVID-19 Pandemic did strike, more than 30% of

[3] https://www.pwc.com/gx/en/issues/crisis-solutions/global-crisis-survey.html

respondents to the 2021 survey did not yet have a designated core crisis response team in place.

PwC comments that organisations need an agile crisis response program that can flex to address various contingencies and types of crises. But only 35% of respondents to the 2021 survey had a crisis response plan that was 'very relevant,' which means the majority did not design their plans to be 'crisis-agnostic', believed to be a hallmark of a resilient organisation.

The second main lesson was the need to further break down silos within the organisation. PwC argues that an integrated response is essential to executing a successful crisis management program and to building resilience. They say that before the COVID-19 Pandemic, many organisations addressed resilience planning as somewhat of a 'spreadsheet exercise', first constructing a Crisis Plan, then a Business Continuity Plan, and then 'Check, check'. This approach exposed many businesses to additional risk as resilience competencies and teams were structured in silos and disjointed, vulnerable and unequipped to coordinate the tactics, tools and technologies needed for an effective response.

The survey showed that seven out of ten organisations were planning to increase their investment in building resilience, with risk officers going as high as nine in ten. Just 23% of respondents felt their various crisis management functions were very well integrated.

The third of the three main lessons identified by respondents to the survey was the need to further strengthen organisational resilience. Seeing resilience as being about being prepared to enable and secure new possibilities as well as the ability to bounce back from disruption and to persevere, PwC argues that organisations have an opportunity in the post-pandemic period to rethink their opportunities for the future. In the survey, three out of four organisations were confident they could successfully integrate what they had learned through the Crisis and invigorate their organisational resilience.

As part of this, they suggest that organisations should establish governance around resilience at the highest level, designating a senior leader to 'sponsor' the resilience program and creating a steering committee to oversee funding and resources. They also argue that there is a need to foster a culture of resilience and position organisational resilience as an umbrella over the organisation's core competencies and across all the technology, operations, data, workforce and financial domains.

But, is this enough? Are there no further lessons to be learnt from the COVID-19 Pandemic in particular, and Global Crises in general, for all organisations, as well as lessons specific to individual ones? Should these not influence the future conduct of our organisations?

At the beginning of this book, in both the Preface and Chapter 1, there are some potential lessons worthy of serious consideration. The Six Fundamental Truths about Crises in the Preface provide a potential basis for a new mindset for organisations after a Global Crisis. Recognising these 'Truths' should be the basis for rethinking our organisational Risk Management, and the need to do that is clearly the most major lesson to be learnt. That is the primary purpose of this book.

To remind you, the 'Truths' state the following:

1. There's going to be another Global Crisis.
2. The next Global Crisis will not be just Financial nor just a pandemic.
3. Current Risk Management is fatally flawed.
4. What we expect often comes to pass.
5. What we don't expect usually doesn't come to pass, until we do expect it to.
6. It will be different next time.

So, the key lesson is to recognise the limitations of our previous organisational mindset and resultant approach, and to reimagine our organisational approaches for the future.

Also, in Chapter 1, we proposed that there are Six Fundamental Reinterpretations of the current Enterprise Risk Management ERM Model that are needed to adequately ensure a sensible reliable useful model. These are also potential 'lessons learnt' that should also affect our organisational mindset and approach. Rephrasing them here, they state the following:

1. Proactively address the systemic gaps in Risk and Continuity Management between operational streams and services.
2. Do not treat all risks as the same; treat Systemic Risks differently.

3. Take a unified holistic view of Business Continuity and Risk.
4. Mobilise early.
5. Protect your organisation from what you cannot conceive.
6. Become Anti-Fragile.

Preparing for the Next Crisis or Should We?

While learning lessons short term is about Recovery, learning lessons long term is about preparing for the next Crisis. As we said above, as our first 'Truth', there is going to be another Global Crisis, so why should we, once again, behave largely as if it is a surprise? Global Crises are normal, arguably with increasing frequency, so it is reasonable that we should prepare our organisation for the next one as soon as the previous Crisis is finishing.

How we should do that is not just a matter of having an Emergency Management and Business Continuity plan. It is not even primarily a question of culture. It is fundamentally about a paradigm shift, and paradigm shifts for organisations are difficult, even more difficult than for individuals. All the stakeholders, including not just the executive and the Board, but also all levels of management and the workforce, need to recognise and accept the new worldview.

The evidence of the need for an organisation to do that is all around it, in the volatility, uncertainty, complexity and ambiguity of the global VUCA environment. But the mechanistic nature of rule-based organisations makes resultant organisational refocus and change difficult. Once an approach or a mindset is established, it can be very hard to change it. It can take a disaster, a Crisis.

As we discussed in Chapter 1, organisations exhibit something of a mixture of the characteristics of human-made and natural systems, with the formal or 'hard' part of the organisation, such as organisational structures, governance rules, management, skills, processes, procedures and technology-based systems, behaving in isolation like mechanistic human-made rule-based systems.

While people, and the resultant culture, leadership, team working, motivation and sense of 'ownership', represent the 'soft' aspects of the organisation, the people aspects of organisations can be both their greatest strengths and their greatest weaknesses. So, in implementing organisational change, we need to work holistically on both systems and cultural aspects.

Thus, in preparing for the next Crisis, and the ones after that, at the people/paradigm level, we need to create a new mindset based on the Six Fundamental Truths about Crises. While, at the systems level, we need simultaneously to consider the Six Fundamental Reinterpretations of the current Enterprise Risk Management ERM Model.

The following and final chapter of this book will consider the implications of these issues further and how to implement a more sensible organisation-level Enterprise Risk Management system that has greater applicability to the current and undoubtedly future VUCA circumstances. Rather than just preparing for the next Crisis, or the one or even ones, after that, by focusing on a new concept of ERM, we are focusing continuous attention on the continuously changing, ebbing and flowing, patterns of risk that each of our organisations faces.

The old, artificially simple, fundamentally static or slow-moving models of risk are no longer even good approximations to the reality of what our organisations are facing. So, it is time for change. The writing on the wall with Risk Management has been there for a long time, but it is now time for change.

8

Implementing Sensible Enterprise Risk Management

Introduction

We argued in the Preface of this book that Risk Management is today both a great success, an impressive achievement, and a notable failure. It works, and it doesn't work. It saves lives and property, and it fails to save lives and property. It helps and it hinders. Like all such management approaches, this has a lot to do with how it is employed and practised but, in the case of Risk Management, there is also a much more fundamental issue. The Risk Management framework, the Risk Management model, is wrong.

We said there that that should not be a surprise, since at best such management formulations reflect the best current thinking on fundamental issues. With time and experience, these are refined and improved taking us closer to the reality that they simplify and represent. Only, in this case, this development, this learning, this growth, has perhaps paused. To make real progress with Risk Management, we now need a fundamental rethink, a paradigm shift. The current Risk Management framework has taken us as far as it can, and it's not far enough to meet our current needs.

Over the last two decades, the desire for a coherent holistic approach to risk across an organisation has been the basis for the emergence of Enterprise Risk Management (ERM) as a new management discipline that calls for companies to identify all the risks they face, to decide which risks to manage actively, and then to make that plan of action available to all stakeholders, rather than just shareholders, as part of their annual reporting. Risk is seen not just as upcoming threats but also in terms of opportunities that may balance them. The release of the Committee of Sponsoring Organisations' (COSO's) ERM Integrated Framework in 2004 did much to establish ERM, and it has now become a business school/MBA discipline.

But ERM has its shortfalls, including being based on a human construct. The practical difficulties in applying it also mean that in reality, although its use has increased worldwide, its application is limited to a relatively small number of organisations, with limited risk coverage, limited holistic formulation and limited effectiveness. For example, a Deloitte & Touche survey back in 2005 found that 45% of organisations had no formal ERM programme, while of the remainder, only 49% had a programme in development and only 6% considered ERM fully operational. Further reporting in 2016 in the Deloitte Global Survey, only 20% of respondents had integrated or optimised their extended Enterprise Risk Management mechanisms.

It is commonly acknowledged that while ERM is conceptually relatively straightforward, its implementation is not. This may mean that an organisation's implementation in practice may have limited coverage of risks, particularly qualitative hard to measure ones, too much emphasis just on defensive regulatory compliance and rubberstamping, limited holistic bringing together of risks from the distinct risk silos, and limited effectiveness. There may also be blame avoidance, an emphasis on time spent filling forms and ticking appropriate boxes, time spent maximising the achievement of target metrics rather than progressing true objectives, and an emphasis on the wrong risks due to disproportionate regulators' or stakeholders' pressure.

Throughout the rest of the book, we then examined the very special circumstances of Global Crises, and how current Risk Management and ERM relate to these. The Conclusion, in general, was 'not well'.

In this final chapter of the book, we now return to the current limitations of Risk Management and ERM. We discuss the continuing flow of global trends and further Black Swans, and we discuss the Objectives and Infrastructure Requirements to implement a more sensible Enterprise Risk Management system. The need to change organisational Corporate Culture and Intent is crucial, and we argue that the role of Government is vital to make substantive progress.

Ongoing Global Trends and Further Black Swans

The World does not appear to be getting any less volatile, uncertain, complex or ambiguous. The VUCA environment is with us for the long term. We still have Grey Rhinoceroses in our organisations, and there will still be Black Swans.

The recognition of Grey Rhinos is now extensive. Michele Wucker, the author of a groundbreaking 2016 book *The Grey Rhino: How to Recognise and Act on the Obvious Dangers We Ignore*, reports President Xi Jinping of China warning of Grey Rhino Risks in January 2019.[1] At the opening ceremony of a study session at the Party School of the CPC Central Committee, he warned senior Communist Party officials that China must be on guard against highly improbable, unimaginable 'black swan' events while also fending off highly probable but often neglected 'grey rhino' risks. Specifically, he said that

> *In the face of a turbulent international situation, a complex and sensitive environment, and the arduous task of reform ... We must be highly vigilant against 'black swan' and 'grey rhinoceros' incidents.*[2]

Some of the Grey Rhinos relate to ongoing global trends that we, and our organisations, are not giving attention to. That is, we are implicitly or explicitly choosing to ignore. Others represent ongoing inbuilt fragilities within our organisations and their environment that, once again, we are effectively blind to, do not acknowledge, and do not deal with.

There are lots of commentators on global trends. In reality, many relate to global circumstances rather than specifically trends, and some concern the combination of both. At the current time, the implications and legacy of the COVID-19 pandemic are a particular set of such circumstances.

One particular set of trends predating the COVID-19 Pandemic are the five global megatrends identified by PwC.[3] These can be presented as follows:

1. Shifting Economic and Political Power
2. Resource Scarcity and Climate Change

---

[1] https://www.wucker.com/tag/gray-rhino/.

[2] http://www.gov.cn/xinwen/2019-01/21/content_5359898.htm.

[3] https://www.pwc.co.uk/issues/megatrends.html.

3. Rapid Urbanisation
4. Technological breakthroughs
5. Changing Demographics

Since such global trends are all intrinsically systemic risks for organisations, it is essential that these are fully understood by the organisation and incorporated into the planning and deployment of the organisational ERM system.

Without such an approach, the organisation is in danger of both ignoring some aspects of these if they are not immediately apparent in brainstorming of potential hazards and, even if they are included, then incorrectly treating them as static risks. As an example, consider Changing Demographics. One easy to neglect aspect of this is the current rapidly ageing population worldwide, which implies, amongst many other serious consequences, that Worldwide, the working-age population (i.e., those aged between 15 to 64 years) will decrease by 10% by 2060. This, in turn, has many serious implications for the organisation, in terms of both workforce and market. Considering this as a static risk is better than ignoring it completely, but still ignores the complexity of risk management needed with systemic risks.

As we discussed in the Preface and Chapter 1, it is often the case that our models of organisational risk management are structured so that they treat systemic risks, the mechanisms of occurrence for big society changing hazards, essentially indifferently from those for the occurrences of routine everyday hazards to the individual organisation so that their separate phases of risk propagation are ignored and the corresponding aggregation sacrifices essential information about the mechanism underlying the big hazard's realisation that undermines effective organisational real-time planning and control. Another consequence of this is potentially downplaying the interconnectivity between risks.

ERM should differentiate the planning and control activities within the phases of a systemic risk, not treat the risk as instantaneous with instantaneous impact. This is true in the context of global trends, as well as global crises. At all levels, systemic risks need to be managed through their distinct phases and ignoring the phases negates the management of the systemic risk, instead treating it as purely an aggregated chance of disaster with an aggregated response to mitigate or manage its effects.

The implication of this is that the structure of Risk Registers should change. No longer should a Risk Register be seen as a monolithic structure in which there is a single crudely uniform approach to risk identification, analysis, evaluation and treatment as defined in ISO 31000, albeit with regular or ongoing monitoring and review of the resultant Risk Register. Instead, separate appropriate infrastructure for the identification of the applicable systemic risks needs to be devised, together with subsequent multiphased analysis, evaluation and treatment.

But there is also considerable variance in the global trends as identified by various commentators. At least partly, these vary with context and purpose. As an example, Gina Westbrook and Alison Angus as authors of the January 2021 'Euromonitor International Top 10 Global Consumer Trends 2021' report focus on emerging and fast-moving global consumer trends that were expected to gain traction in the year ahead.[4] These trends were identified to provide insight into changing consumer values, exploring how consumer behaviour was shifting and causing disruption for businesses globally. Such customer trends are, of course, a subset of global trends, albeit an important one, but still represent potential systemic risks to organisations. Examples are the returning consumer emphasis on environmental impact post-COVID and the increasing drive for convenience.

Also writing in January 2021, Shubham Singhal of McKinsey saw 2021 as the 'year of transition' and defines trends that they say 'will shape the next normal' and 'define 2021 — and beyond'.[5] These include the return of confidence unleashing a consumer rebound, pandemic-induced changes in shopping behaviour forever altering consumer businesses, leisure travel bouncing back while business travel lags, the COVID-19 crisis sparking a wave of innovation and launching a generation of entrepreneurs, digitally enabled productivity gains accelerating the Fourth Industrial Revolution, supply chains rebalancing and shifting, working from home and adapting

[4] https://www.euromonitor.com/article/what-are-the-2021-top-10-global-consumer-trends.

[5] https://www.mckinsey.com/featured-insights/leadership/the-next-normal-arrives-trends-that-will-define-2021-and-beyond.

the workforce to the requirements of automation and digitisation accelerated, portfolio restructuring accelerating, Green becoming the colour of recovery, governments addressing their fiscal difficulties through possibly raising taxes and cutting spending, and the increasing prominence of stakeholder capitalism.

In the context of International Development, Mikaela Gavas and Samuel Pleeck writing in March 2021 in a policy note prepared at the request of Norwegian Ministry for Foreign Affairs in support of its Global Trends Initiative, look at global trends in 2021.[6]

They argue that while most of the world is still in the midst of the COVID-19 pandemic, a few basic aspects of the new global context are easy to identify, even if their specific consequences are still speculative. They review and overlay some of the features of the COVID crisis on earlier observed trends and dynamics and explore some of the changes and trends in development agency strategic direction brought about by the pandemic. The implications of what this study shows will clearly be systemic risks for some organisations. For example, they project unequal economic recovery with a steep decline in global trade and financial flows to developing countries. They also identify reversed progress in global poverty reduction and human development, and amplified inequalities, including in gender and digital accessibility. Furthermore, they identify strengthened forces of rivalry, anti-globalisation, nationalism, and vaccine apartheid.

Other global trends are identified by the Office of the Director of US National Intelligence.[7] Published in March 2021, the 7th edition of the National Intelligence Council's Global Trends report which has been published every four years since 1997 assesses the key trends and uncertainties that it is believed will shape the strategic environment for the United States during the next two decades.

The analysis is in three general sections. First, structural forces are analysed in the four core areas of demographics, environment, economics, and technology. These areas are selected because they are foundational in

[6] 'Global Trends in 2021: How COVID-19 is Transforming International Development', Centre for Global Development, March 2 2021, https://www.cgdev.org/publication/global-trends-2021-how-covid-transforming-international-development.

[7] https://www.dni.gov/index.php/gt2040-home/summary/the-covid-factor; https://www.dni.gov/files/ODNI/documents/assessments/GlobalTrends_2040.pdf.

shaping future dynamics and relatively universal in scope, and projections can be identified with a reasonable degree of confidence based on available data and evidence.

The second section examines how these structural forces interact and intersect with other factors to affect emerging dynamics at the three levels of individuals and society, states, and the international system. The analysis in this section involves a higher degree of uncertainty because of the variability of human choices to be made in the future. Focus is on identifying and describing the key emerging dynamics at each level, including what is driving them and how they might evolve over time.

Finally, the third section identifies several key uncertainties and uses these to create five future scenarios for the world in 2040. These scenarios are not predictions but widen the aperture as to the possibilities, exploring various combinations of how the structural forces, emerging dynamics, and key uncertainties could play out.

The COVID-19 pandemic that emerged globally in 2020 has wreaked havoc across the world disrupting economies and political dynamics within and between countries, as well as, killing millions of people and devastating communities. Whilst previous Global Trends editions forecasted the potential for new diseases and even imagined scenarios with a pandemic, they lacked a full picture of the breadth and depth of its disruptive potential. COVID-19 has shaken long-held assumptions about resilience and adaptation and created new uncertainties about the economy, governance, geopolitics, and technology.

Accordingly, to understand and assess the impact of this Crisis, the Office of the Director of US National Intelligence has examined a broad range of prior assumptions and assessments related to key global trends. Questions asked included the following:

> Which existing trends will endure, which trends are accelerating or decelerating because of the pandemic, and where are we likely to experience fundamental, systemic shifts?
>
> Are the disruptions temporary or could the pandemic unleash new forces to shape the future?

They argue that much like the terrorist attacks of 11 September 2001, the COVID-19 pandemic is likely to produce some changes that will be felt for years to come and change the way we live, work, and govern domestically and internationally. Furthermore, they argue that the pandemic and corresponding national responses appear to be honing and accelerating several trends that were already underway before the outbreak. Accordingly, these represent intrinsically systemic risks and opportunities for organisations.

For example, lockdowns, quarantines, and the closing of international borders have catalysed some pre-existing economic trends, whilst there is reinforcement of nationalism and polarisation, deepening inequality, straining governance, failures in international cooperation and an elevated role for non-state actors, including some private sector organisations.

In contrast, COVID-19 is also slowing and possibly reversing some longstanding trends in human development, especially the reduction of poverty and disease and closing of gender inequality gaps.

As we discussed above, some of the Grey Rhinos within our organisations relate to ongoing global trends like the above that we, and our organisations, are not giving attention to. At the same time, consensus on these trends is far from universal. Other Grey Rhinos represent ongoing inbuilt fragilities within our organisations and their environment that we are effectively blind to, do not acknowledge, and do not deal with. An example of both may be until relatively recently, the potential impacts of climate change.

For a number of years, Michele Wucker prepared an annual list of the then current Top 10 Grey Rhinos near the end of the first quarter of each year so that she could capture a global sense of the top risks and prediction lists for the year, and then circle back mid-year and as the year closed, to see how these risks — and our responses — had progressed. For 2020, her top five grey rhino risks that emerged from her meta-analysis of dozens of the years' top risks, predictions, and outlook lists were the following[8]:

1. Economic and financial fragilities
2. Political uncertainty, both domestic and geo-political
3. Climate change

4. Cyber and digital risk
5. Supply chain risks.[8]

A full approach to Risk Management needs to differentiate the planning and control activities within the phases of a systemic risk, not treat the risk as instantaneous with instantaneous impact. At all levels, systemic risks need to be managed through their distinct phases and ignoring the phases negates the management of the systemic risk, instead treating it as purely an aggregated chance of disaster with an aggregated response to mitigate or manage its effects. Accordingly, the structure of Risk Registers should change from monolithic structures in which there is a single crudely uniform approach to risk identification, analysis, evaluation and treatment, to separate appropriate infrastructure for the identification of applicable systemic risks, together with subsequent multiphased analysis, evaluation and treatment.

But there will be ongoing surprises of Black Swans also in our VUCA environment, and a rethinking of risk management needs to deal with these too, as well as Global Trends and Grey Rhinos. Of these three categories of systemic risks, it is Black Swans that is potentially most problematic to structurally include in a rethought and more sensible Enterprise Risk Management system because the evidence of their existence is far from easily accessible *pre hoc*.

There are, however, three apparent easy mitigations for this issue. One is the mandatory identification and application of precautionary principles appropriate to the organisation's context. The second is the addition of mandatory horizon scanning as a preliminary stage in Risk Identification. And the third is the appropriate categorisation of potential Black Swan Events according to their intrinsic characteristics and mechanisms, rather than treating them as a generic class of risks, so as to facilitate appropriate dedicated phased precautions, monitoring and treatment. We shall consider the application of these three mitigations in the next section.

Here though, we shall first consider further the continuing flow of global Black Swans. Nassim N. Taleb, Daniel G. Goldstein, and Mark

[8] https://www.thegrayrhino.com/the-top-gray-rhinos-of-2020/.

W. Spitznagel, writing in *The Harvard Review* in 2009, commented the following:

> *We don't live in the world for which conventional risk-management textbooks prepare us. No forecasting model predicted the impact of the current economic crisis, and its consequences continue to take establishment economists and business academics by surprise.*
>
> Nassim N. Taleb, Daniel G. Goldstein, and Mark W. Spitznagel, The Six Mistakes Executives Make in Risk Management, *The Harvard Review*, October 2009.[9]

They go on to say the following:

> *Low-probability, high-impact events that are almost impossible to forecast — we call them Black Swan events — are increasingly dominating the environment. Because of the internet and globalisation, the world has become a complex system, made up of a tangled web of relationships and other interdependent factors. Complexity not only increases the incidence of Black Swan events but also makes forecasting even ordinary events impossible. All we can predict is that companies that ignore Black Swan events will go under.*

Very relevant to our arguments here, these authors conclude the following:

> ***Instead of trying to anticipate low-probability, high-impact events, we should reduce our vulnerability to them. Risk management, we believe, should be about lessening the impact of what we don't understand*** *— not a futile attempt to develop sophisticated techniques and stories that perpetuate our illusions of being able to understand and predict the social and economic environment.*

They then identify six mistakes that need to be avoided in undertaking Risk Management. These can be summarised as follows:

1. Attempting to manage risk by predicting extreme events.
2. Attempting to manage risk by studying the past and looking to identify 'typical' hazards we might expect.

[9] https://hbr.org/2009/10/the-six-mistakes-executives-make-in-risk-management.

3. Focusing on 'business as usual' and the upside of risks and paying insufficient attention to avoiding exposure to risks through limiting risky activities.
4. Assuming that risks can be measured in terms of standard deviations.
5. Failing to pay attention to the presentation and psychological context of risk, which means that the same risk may be accepted or avoided depending on how it is presented.
6. Not understanding that efficiency causes fragility, that redundancy can help protect against this, and that rewarding upsides without penalising downsides is very dangerous.

Though the authors do not raise it, point four also reflects a more general issue that summarising risk in terms of any such summary measures, or expectations, is inappropriate as with risk it is the single extreme individual occurrence that we need to protect against the impact of, not the average expectation.

Objectives and Infrastructure Requirements

What then are the key ingredients for Objectives and Infrastructure Requirements to implement a more sensible reimagined Enterprise Risk Management system? Considering first the Objectives, what are, and what should be, the objectives of an organisational ERM implementation?

In Chapter 1, we argued that ERM is the best approach to managing organisational risk we have today, but there are currently many things wrong with the practice of Enterprise Risk Management, particularly when we think in terms of Global Crises. In Chapter 1 and the Preface, we specifically identified many shortcomings, such as not including Black Swans or risks you cannot conceive, being difficult to implement, and in practice having limited effectiveness. In the context of Global Crises, ERM typically does not give adequate attention to the difference in nature of systemic risks, such as global trends, grey rhinos and black swans, and the need to treat them differently from local risks.

These shortcomings reflect the differences between what are currently, and what should be, the objectives of an organisational ERM implementation. According to COSO, currently, the objectives of an organisational ERM implementation are based on the following statement:

> *The underlying premise of enterprise risk management is that every entity exists to provide value for its stakeholders. All entities face uncertainty, and the challenge for management is to determine how much uncertainty to accept as it strives to grow stakeholder value. Uncertainty presents both risk and opportunity, with the potential to erode or enhance value.* ***Enterprise risk management enables management to effectively deal with uncertainty and associated risk and opportunity, enhancing the capacity to build value.***
>
> *Value is maximised when management sets strategy and objectives to strike an optimal balance between growth and return goals and related risks, and efficiently and effectively deploys resources in pursuit of the entity's objectives.*

Enterprise Risk Management — Integrated Framework Executive Summary, COSO September 2004.[10]

In contrast, Investopedia[11] defines key takeaways as follows:

- Enterprise risk management (ERM) is a firm-wide strategy to identify and prepare for hazards with a company's finances, operations, and objectives.
- ERM allows managers to shape the firm's overall risk position by mandating certain business segments engage with or disengage from particular activities.
- Traditional risk management, which leaves decision-making in the hands of division heads, can lead to siloed evaluations that do not account for other divisions.
- ERM techniques have evolved substantially over the last decades.

It is also recognised that an organisational enterprise risk management framework is geared to achieving the organisation's strategic, operational, reporting and compliance objectives.

However, while broadly appropriate, the high-level objectives of ERM on their own fail to adequately capture the mechanisms needed to enable organisational management to effectively deal with uncertainty and associated risk and opportunity within the current global

[10] https://www.coso.org/documents/coso-erm-executive-summary.pdf.

[11] https://www.investopedia.com/terms/e/enterprise-risk-management.asp.

environment. What is needed, in addition, is explicit objectives for the ERM implementation that enable management to effectively deal with uncertainty and associated risk and opportunity, **within the full dynamics of the VUCA environment**, rather than on a historic prior assumption of stability. In particular, any organisational ERM implementation needs to appropriately address systemic risks rather than treating them as point events. Properly addressing such systemic risks, including global trends, grey rhinos and black swans, should, by definition, be the primary purpose of an organisational ERM system.

Thus, any organisation's ERM system should be explicitly and adequately designed to do the job such systems purport to do. Unfortunately, to date, they do not. Moving from this structure will require changes to the infrastructure of many organisational ERM systems.

Typical organisational ERM systems today essentially treat the risk register largely the same as in ISO 31000. Risks are identified and rated on likelihood and severity, as the basis for prioritisation and treatment. Sometimes, in addition, ERM systems include Risk Velocity as a third dimension of a risk, largely representing its potential 'time to impact'. In any event, what is in the risk register is a gross simplification of an organisation's reality.

In the 'Enterprise Risk Management — Integrated Framework' COSO 2014, it is stated as follows:

> *Events can have negative impact, positive impact, or both.* ***Events with a negative impact represent risks****, which can prevent value creation or erode existing value. Events with positive impact may offset negative impacts or represent opportunities. Opportunities are the possibility that an event will occur and positively affect the achievement of objectives, supporting value creation or preservation. Management channels opportunities back to its strategy or objective-setting processes, formulating plans to seize the opportunities.*

An improved approach to ERM requires a new approach, and new infrastructure, for the risk register. Instead of a focus on **events** representing risks, hence implicitly excluding or summarising the complex interwoven causal paths associated with systemic risks, systemic risks such as global crises, grey rhinos, black swans or dangerous global trends need to be seen as **dynamic paths**.

Moreover, associating an impact, likelihood and possibly velocity with the event further over-summarises any systemic risk, since the reality for many such risks is a small probability or likelihood of a high impact while at the same time a high likelihood of a smaller impact. For example, there may be a higher likelihood of a small impact weather occurrence, compared to a large impact weather occurrence.

Artificially reducing the underlying two-dimensional distribution to a single summarising point in the two-dimensional range is, at best, extremely dangerous. Perhaps at worst, it could be said to introduce systematic bias in underestimating risk, by introducing some averaging into the definition of the likelihood and impact of risks themselves.

Hence, the traditional ERM risk register, together with the mechanisms of risk management and control, needs reimagining in the context of the VUCA environment and systemic events, such as global crises. For these, an extended risk register framework is needed. What are its characteristics? To answer this question, we can now return to the phased nature of global crises that we discussed previously in this book.

It may be argued in general that at any one time, an organisation will be facing a portfolio of risks. Included in this portfolio may be some 'conventional' 'point event risks', such as financial over-exposure or loss of business. While even these, in reality, have dynamic paths and may be systemic, in practice they may be well approximated by conventional risk analysis. If such approximation is safely possible, it should be utilised in the interests of parsimony.

As well as these 'fixed point event' risks, however, there will be at any time a probably extensive range of dynamic systemic risks that, for safety, should not be treated as the same. For these, rather than summarising them in terms of a perhaps arbitrary 'average' impact and likelihood, there is a need to consider their dynamic mechanisms in propagation. As we discussed in the Preface, with systemic risks, once an initiating event occurs, a sequence unravels whereby modest 'tipping points' combine indirectly to produce large failures, 'contagion' occurs as one loss triggers a chain of others and then 'hysteresis' occurs, with systems being unable to recover equilibrium after a shock.

For example, with a Global Crisis, following the initiating event, or at the end of this initiation sequence, the Crisis has reached such a magnitude that its impending threat is now substantially visible, and it now progresses further through its phases to unfold to Crisis Point, when the anticipated maximum danger and threat is realised.

In line with the six fundamental reinterpretations needed for the current ERM Model that we identified in Chapter 1, let us now consider the required infrastructure for dealing suitably with such systemic risks, taking a Global Crisis, such as the COVID-19 Pandemic, as an example.

As we discussed in Chapter 1, early in the COVID-19 Crisis, despite

- clear warning of the next global pandemic going back at least a decade,
- early warning of the emerging threat within China at the start of 2020,
- explicit evidence of the pandemic starting to spread internationally,
- clear emergence into a global phenomenon, and subsequently,
- development into a severe local threat,

little organisational attention was given to it, or responsive actions instigated, by many organisations for many months until instructed or asked to do so by central government authority as 'the fat hit the pan' at the last of the above phases.

Accordingly, in Figure 8.1, we show an example comparison of the likely responses to a Global Crisis, such as the COVID-19 pandemic, utilising a conventional organisational ERM risk register and an idealised Systemic Risk-based one.

The response to the Crisis from the idealised systemic risk-based ERM approach is clearly potentially vastly superior. It follows that the Infrastructure Requirements to implement a more sensible Enterprise Risk Management system need to include a risk register containing progressively phased systemic risks based on the best available information and judgement and incorporating progressive precautionary principles. The easy to implement and interpret Impact/Likelihood risk register is also a grossly inaccurate and inadequate one in a VUCA environment and so needs to be replaced.

In order to differentiate the planning and control activities within the phases of a systemic risk, not treat the risk as instantaneous with

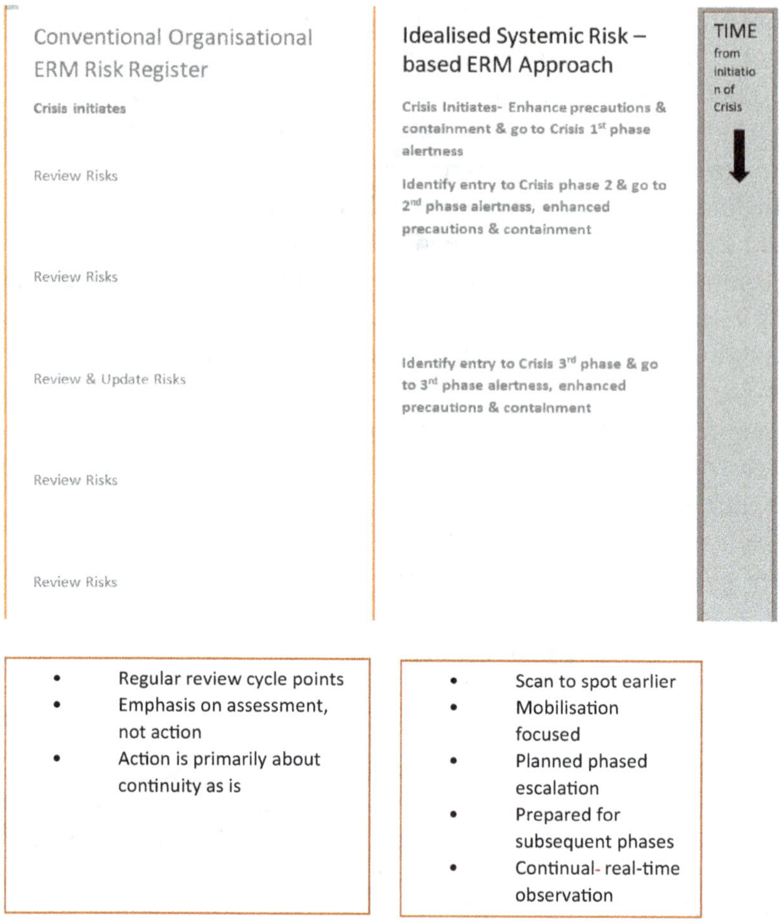

Figure 8.1. An Example Comparison of Responses to a Global Crisis, such as the COVID-19 Pandemic, Utilising a Conventional Organisational ERM Risk Register and an Idealised Systemic Risk-Based One.

instantaneous impact, the structure of Risk Registers should change from monolithic structures in which there is a single crudely uniform approach to risk identification, analysis, evaluation and treatment, to separate appropriate infrastructure for the identification of applicable systemic risks, together with subsequent multiphased analysis, evaluation and treatment.

The form of replacement can vary with organisational and environmental circumstances rather than of necessity being squeezed into an alternative predefined over-summarised format. Its content, however, remains clear; it's an ongoing map of the organisation's risks, which at a given point of time identifies the potential phased levels of each identified risk stretching forward, including, as appropriate, likelihood and impact.

In the previous section of this chapter, we said that, of course, there will be ongoing surprises of Black Swans in our VUCA environment, and a rethinking of risk management needs to deal with these too, as well as Global Trends and Grey Rhinos. Of the three, it is Black Swans that are potentially most problematic to structurally include in a rethought and more sensible Enterprise Risk Management system because the evidence of their existence is far from easily accessible *pre hoc*. We talked thereof the following three apparent easy mitigations for this issue:

a. The mandatory identification and application of precautionary principles appropriate to the organisation's context.
b. The addition of mandatory horizon scanning as a preliminary stage in Risk Identification.
c. The appropriate categorisation of potential Black Swan Events according to their intrinsic characteristics and mechanisms rather than treating them as a generic class of risks, so as to facilitate appropriate dedicated phased precautions, monitoring and treatment.

Each of these three mitigations represents an important component of the reimagined ERM approach suitable for a VUCA environment. Generally, incorporating them into ERM practice within an organisation will necessitate considerably more thought than in current practice, but they are major safeguards. Each should be an ongoing process incorporating constant review.

It would be good to see organisations publishing their key list of current precautionary principles and 'never events' as part of their annual reports. This would provide stakeholders with the basis to evaluate both aspirations and practice to hold their governing bodies to account, as well as provide some safeguards against Black Swans.

The inclusion of systematic horizon scanning will also provide some such protection, but its effectiveness will be highly correlated with the extensiveness of its scope. The current ERM infrastructure and mindset, as discussed previously, may lead to risk blindness in certain crucial dimensions.

The third mitigation is perhaps the most novel. The categorisation of Black Swans to date has remained limited, reflecting their low probabilities, unpredictability and potentially enormous impacts. Classifying potential Black Swan events according to their intrinsic characteristics and particularly mechanisms, rather than treating them as a generic class of risks, will, however, facilitate some appropriate dedicated phased precautions, monitoring and treatment.

For example, in broad terms, we might think of the following major Black Swan categories:

- global pandemics
- financial crises
- political instability
- technological failure
- ecosystem collapse

These can, of course, be specialised to more specific subcategories of Black Swan risks, with generally dedicated phased precautions, monitoring and treatment becoming more effective, the more specific the defined risk. Considering the organisation's value streams and a PESTEL analysis of the environment provides good potential input. And, in turn, this can form the basic structure for horizon scanning.

Corporate Culture and Intent

It is a truism that the biggest risk to any organisation is the organisation itself. Organisations lose their way, take their eye off the ball, do not stay alert, take on too much, don't manage their stakeholders, don't see the writing on the wall, don't really know what they are doing or the world they are in, fail to see that the world is changing, and fail to adequately manage risk.

A sensible new approach to ERM in any organisation needs to make that realisation conscious, visual, compelling, immediate, constant and continually acted upon. Risk is part of life; we should not see it as an add-on. But we have history, legacy, and established paradigms, and these make it much harder to navigate. Typically, within all organisations, existing infrastructure reflects past circumstances and needs, and that means they reflect the pre-VUCA environment and thinking, which is far from good from a risk perspective.

And there is explicit and implicit resistance to change in our structures, as inertias and balancing loops, as well as some people, work to maintain the status quo.

So, as an organisation, we start with our people at all levels having a limited understanding of risk in relation to our business. We try to deal with this by having named officers with risk responsibilities. We put in rigid systems, and we chase certificates, but on many occasions, we miss the point. Don't we?

The fundamental issue here is the reimagining of our work. Remember risk is not an add-on, risk is intrinsic to life. If you are alive, then you are exposed to risk, and if you want to remain fully alive with all your faculties, family and possessions, then considering, managing and optimising risk is 100% part of your daily activities. Just as it should be for organisations. Perhaps just as with an irresponsible adolescent, the organisation itself is the biggest risk to that organisation if it does not do this.

Superimposed on this are Groupthink and culture. Groupthink represents an abdication of personal responsibility when faced with a common consensus. Essentially, it is a psychological phenomenon that occurs within a group of people in which the desire for harmony or conformity in the group results in an irrational or dysfunctional decision-making outcome. Perhaps we support the corporate view, or the established norm, no matter what.

Cohesiveness, or the desire for cohesiveness, in a group may produce a tendency among its members to agree at all costs. This can cause the group to minimise conflict and reach a consensus decision without critical evaluation. During the early stages of the Financial Crisis, with the emphasis on the upside, did many corporate bankers suffer from Groupthink and downplay the risks?

Because of long legacies within organisations, and because the VUCA environment in contrast is very much a recent phenomenon, does our current organisational culture reflect a somewhat historic circumstance, from a world which was less joined-up and hence less Volatile, Uncertain, Complex and Ambiguous? Of course, to some extent at least, it does.

So, core to the reimagining and implementing of a sensible ERM system suitable for our VUCA environment is the need, not just to make everyone risk-aware, not just to change our organisational culture, but to refocus our organisational intent, our systems, our people, our value streams and supply chains onto considering, managing and optimising risk as being 100% part of our strategic and daily activities.

To do this is a strategic, educational and communication challenge. But in a VUCA world, it is necessary. Changing people in this way, and our organisational culture, will take time and perseverance. It will take 'bottle'. And we will need continual vigilance. Being risk-aware is about never quite relaxing, always watching, questioning, evaluating, and standing ready. Such are the demands of the VUCA world.

The Role of Government

Throughout this book, we have focused primarily on rethinking risk management to survive future global crises, from the perspective of an individual organisation. While much of what we have discussed is applicable to public sector organisations also, our emphasis has primarily been on the private sector. However, the very nature of the VUCA environment with its hyper-interconnectivity means that the fate of an organisation will partially depend on the actions and inactions of external players, as well as internal ones. Of these, perhaps the most major potential role is that of national government.

The actions of governments will affect the survivability of organisations in Global Crises both directly and indirectly. Direct actions include those such as furlough schemes, subsidies, mandatory or voluntary lockdowns, and their timings and durations potentially impact all resident organisations. More indirect actions, like international trade disputes, Brexit and tax reforms, also have an impact.

Having discussed how an organisation can prepare and manage itself better to survive future Global Crises, let's now look at what the role of Government should be. To frame this role, let us recognise that as we discussed in the Preface, a Global Crisis, by definition, threatens the continuity of our society, our economy and our way of life. Given this, and the recognition of the increased magnitude and frequency of such danger associated with the VUCA environment, any residual view that Government should not perhaps accept this role is largely untenable.

If Government, therefore, is to accept this role, it should discharge it with maximum effectiveness. Unfortunately, however, just as organisations have failed to be close to being fully prepared for the VUCA environment and Global Crises and effectively manage through them, clearly, so have governments.

Since Government carries leadership responsibility and typically represents the primary basis for aligned decisive action, it carries not just a responsive duty of care through a Crisis but a requirement for timely, proactive Crisis Management. And in broad terms, it has the connections and resources to discharge this. However, arguably, the recognition of this grave responsibility, like the understanding of how it should be discharged with maximum effectiveness, is not yet anywhere near firmly established.

There are many ways that Government action could help organisations, as well as citizens, thrive in the VUCA world and survive Global Crises. The basic precepts for many of the areas of intervention are immediately apparent but neglected. In many senses, they represent facing up to aspects of the most serious Grey Rhinos that world society today faces.

Apart from direct support actions, such as furlough schemes and subsidies, there are a considerable number of structural actions that would support organisational survival. The following are some examples:

Education of Citizens

Globally, the COVID-19 Crisis revealed the disturbing extent to which some citizens were not able to identify and correctly evaluate sources of information and misinformation, which then impacted their actions, which adversely affected other individuals, institutions and organisations. For some, social media postings of extreme Anti-Vax conspiracy theories were given greater credibility than evidence-based peer-reviewed information from reliable, verifiable, legitimate sources.

Underlying Grey Rhinos here are the gross failure of our education systems globally to adequately provide the most basic essential life skills for all our citizens to be able to source and validate appropriate information and data, and the time lag between the emergence of new technology, in the form of social media, and the catch up of law and regulation.

A related issue is the deep failure of many citizens to understand the intrinsic nature of risk. A recent good start is that communities around the world are now participating in a project to develop a framework for 'risk know-how', the Risk Know-How Framework supported by the Institute for the Public Understanding of Risk at the University of Singapore and the Lloyds Register Foundation ('What is Risk Know-How?' Tracey Brown, Significance Dec 2021, Vol 18 Issue 6, pp 30–35). However, there remains an enormous amount to do in this regard.

Government action in terms of education in this field, on a precautionary basis now, would be likely to reduce harmful impacts in future Global Crises, for organisations as well as citizens, particularly as, as we discussed in Chapter 1, the multiplier effect in contagion here is human behaviour.

Education of Organisations

There is also an extended educational need for organisations, particularly SMEs, building on previous government support programmes worldwide. For example, one important Grey Rhino is that while the drive to efficiency has led to geographically extended supply chains, this in turn has led to particularly fragile ones, as, once again, COVID-19 has demonstrated.

An understanding of the VUCA nature of our world, and its consequential risks, is imperative to business. Government action here should be at multiple levels: directly targeted education programmes and support for SMEs, work with Business Schools defining new curriculum, collection of case studies showing successful adaption and management, and support for the development of new models of organisational excellence that go beyond the limitations of the models, such as the EFQM, Baldrige and Deming Prize, that were developed in the pre-VUCA period.

Improving Board Governance

Globally, limitations of Board Governance have led to ongoing failures of organisations that tend to increase greatly in Global Crises. This is a Grey

Figure 8.2. Basis for Board Scrutiny (based on EFQM)

Rhino, BUT alas, here, we have a potential stampede of Grey Rhinos! As an author, I have been vocal for many years about a number of these. Relevant contributing and interrelated Grey Rhinos here include the following:

- Frequently, Board members, and sometimes whole Boards, do not fully understand their statutory and business obligations to effectively scrutinise and help improve aspects of the organisation and their Board role. See Figure 8.2.
- A lack of clarity and vision on the Board's role and purposes, often bureaucratic mindsets and the organisation's Executive Management's *de facto* control of primary information access for the Board.
- The Board may see itself or may act as having a more limited remit than its statutory and business responsibilities and the above model presents. In particular, it may limit its focus and vision primarily to day-to-day operations and planned developments. Hence, it may give detailed consideration to Management Accounts, Budgets, Cash flow, Sales data and historic Customer Information in pursuit of deciding 'Will it be OK?', with the only attention to the Environment being to Interest Rates. Thus, it assumes continuity and duplicates the work of management.

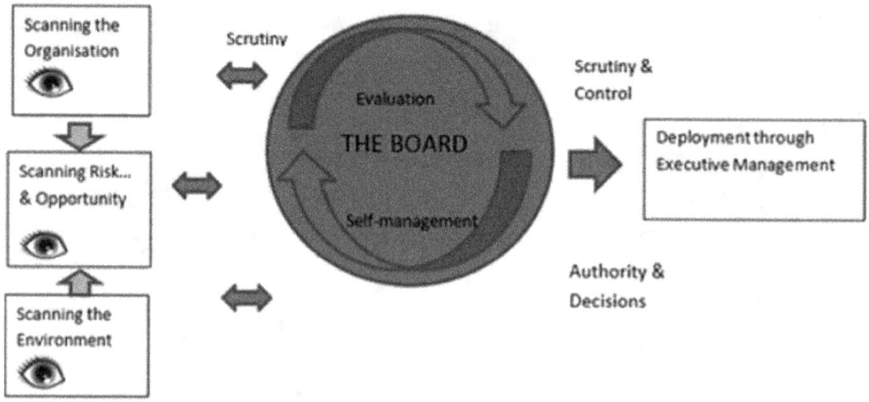

Figure 8.3. The Real, But Potentially Unrealised, Role of the Board

- Shortfalls in the health of the Board may reflect directly ERM-related issues, such as not identifying risk and opportunity effectively, nor acting on these, an apparent inability to make things happen, the lack of access to necessary information, nor the ability to process it effectively, or it seeing itself as having a more limited remit than its statutory and business responsibilities present.
- Capacity is another key issue. Does the Board necessarily have the range and depth of skills required for its tasks? Do the Board members have the clarity of purpose, dedication, and resources to do the job? Does the Chair need help in assessing the current Board and member capacity, and in developing it further to meet needs?

The potential for Government intervention in terms of improving Board Governance is again at multiple levels, including both education and regulation. See Figure 8.3.

Real-time Information Management

The COVID-19 pandemic has, again, brought into view a group of crucial Grey Rhinos at the Government, as well as organisational, level. Broadly, these can be summarised in terms of a mismatch between legacy data systems and the need for real-time information management to support necessary actions. This showed, e.g., in the cycle times in the UK's tracking of National Health Service data.

Government action here to support proper data analytics and its own and organisations' activities, is again potentially at multiple levels.

Ownership or partnering on key logistics infrastructure

Of course, yet another Grey Rhino revealed by recent events during the pandemic concerns the fragility of extended supply chains based on the lowest price. Apart from this being an area where Government intervention in terms of SME education would be highly helpful, it should also draw attention to the related issue, or Grey Rhino, of the concentration of ownership and potential shortage of key logistics infrastructure, such as container ships.

Here too is a potentially crucial area where more immediate Government structural action can support organisational survival through future Global Crises so that this might be seen, similar to the argument for strategic infrastructure in previous eras, as a key precautionary principle at the national level. Ownership or long-term strategic crisis-partnering can be an option with different pros and cons, but the dominance of political dogma predating the VUCA-environment may represent a further Grey Swan, preventing action.

Bibliography

Preface

Atkins *et al.* (2011). Roads to ruin study report, Cass Business School. https://www.airmic.com/sites/default/files/technical-documents/Roads-to-Ruin-the-analysis.pdf.

Cambridge English Dictionary Definition of a Crisis. https://dictionary.cambridge.org/dictionary/english/crisis.

Collins English Dictionary Definition of a Global Crisis. https://www.collinsdictionary.com/dictionary/english/global-crisis.

Committee of Sponsoring Organisations (COSOs). (2004). ERM Integrated Framework.

Deloitte & Touche LLP & Committee of Chief Risk Officers. (2005). Enterprise Risk Management Survey.

Jasper Fforde, Expectation Influenced Probability. See, e.g., https://www.significancemagazine.com/culture/80-the-weight-of-expectations-jasper-fforde.

ISO 31000: 2018 'Risk management — Guidelines'.

Lexology. (23 March, 2020). https://www.lexology.com/library/detail.aspx?g=31160b44-ac35-4249-adca-e69416ff3819.

Oxford English Dictionary alternative definition of Risk. https://www.oed.com/.

Wikipedia Definition of Crisis. https://en.wikipedia.org/wiki/Crisis.

Chapter 1

Ackoff Russell L. (February, 1979). The future of operational research is past. *The Journal of the Operational Research Society*, 30(2), 93–104.

Checkland P. (2010). *Systems Thinking, Systems Practice.* New York: Springer Science and Business Media.

Churchman C. W. (1971). *The Design of Inquiring Systems: Basic Concepts of Systems and Organisation.* New York: Basic Books.

Churchman C. W. (1979). *The Systems Approach and Its Enemies.* New York: Basic Books.

David Peter Stroh. A systems view of the economic crisis. https://thesystemsthinker.com/a-systems-view-of-the-economic-crisis/.

Donella Meadows Leverage Points; Places to Intervene in a System, The Sustainability Institute (1999). http://www.donellameadows.org/wp-content/userfiles/Leverage_Points.pdf.

Geary Sikich. https://accendoreliability.com/black-swans-grey-swans-white-swans/.

Mark Carney, invited commentary about the current Global Crisis; how the economy must yield to human values, *The Economist* (16 April, 2020). https://www.economist.com/by-invitation/2020/04/16/mark-carney-on-how-the-economy-must-yield-to-human-values.

Nassim Nicholas Taleb. (2010). *The Black Swan: The Impact of the Highly Improbable 2007.* 2nd ed. Penguin. London.

See, e.g., Jasper Fforde (2012). *One of Our Thursdays is Missing*, Hodder (2012) and https://www.significancemagazine.com/culture/80-the-weight-of-expectations-jasper-fforde. Published by Hodder & Stroughton, London.

Wikipedia entry on the Matrix (franchise). https://en.wikipedia.org/wiki/The_Matrix_(franchise).

Chapter 2

(12 May, 2020). https://www.forbes.com/sites/laurelfarrer/2020/05/12/the-new-normal-isnt-remote-work-its-better/#3fcf69fb2405.

(May, 2020). http://www.erm360.com/erm-process/the-chief-risk-officer/.

(May, 2020). https://en.wikipedia.org/wiki/Chief_risk_officer.

(May, 2020). https://www.investopedia.com/terms/c/chief-risk-officer-cro.asp.

Bendell Tony. (2014). *Building Anti-Fragile Organisations: Risk, Opportunity and Governance in a Turbulent World.* Farnham: Gower.

Chief Risk Officer: What is a CRO? (and Why You Need One) by Juliana De Grout on Tuesday 18 September, 2018. https://digitalguardian.com/blog/chief-risk-officer-what-cro-and-why-you-need-one.

https://resources.infosecinstitute.com/job-titles/business-continuity-manager/#gref.

ISO 22301: 2019 'Security and Resilience — Business Continuity Management Systems — Requirements'.

ISO 31000: 2018 'Risk management — Guidelines'.

Michele Wucker Stop Calling the Coronavirus Outbreak a Black Swan (27 January, 2020). https://www.thegrayrhino.com/stop-calling-the-coronavirus-outbreak-a-black-swan/.

Michele Wucker. (2016). *The Grey Rhino: How to Recognise and Act on the Obvious Dangers We Ignore*. St Martin's Press. London.

Risk Management job description guide— Robert Half (January, 2022). https://www.roberthalf.com.au/employers/financial-services/risk-management-jobs.

Risk Manager Job Description. (May, 2020). https://resources.workable.com/risk-manager-job-description.

Chapter 3

Federation of American Scientists (FAS). The Intelligence Cycle in the context of US National Security. https://fas.org/irp/cia/product/facttell/intcycle.htm.

Gartner. https://www.gartner.com/en/documents/2487216/definition-threat-intelligence.

Technical Specification PD CEN/TS 17091:2018. (2018). *Crisis Management — Guidance for Developing a Strategic Capability*. Publisher: BSI, London.

UK Terror Threat Levels. (2006). https://www.mi5.gov.uk/threat-levels.

US National Terrorism Advisory System (NTAS). (2011). Department of Homeland Security. https://www.dhs.gov/national-terrorism-advisory-system.

World Health Organisation (WHO). (1999 revised 2005, 2009 & 2013). Influenza pandemic phase classification. https://www.who.int/influenza/preparedness/pandemic/PIRM_update_052017.pdf.

Chapter 4

OECD Policy Responses. (June, 2020). The impact of the coronavirus (COVID-19) crisis on development finance. http://www.oecd.org/coronavirus/policy-responses/the-impact-of-the-coronavirus-covid-19-crisis-on-development-finance-9de00b3b/.

The Fishbowl Format. Decision making in uncertain times, McKinsey (24 March, 2020). https://www.mckinsey.com/business-functions/organization/our-insights/decision-making-in-uncertain-times.

Chapter 5

BS 67000: 2019 'City resilience — Guide'.

Committee of Sponsoring Organizations ERM Integrated Framework. (2004). https://www.coso.org/pages/erm-integratedframework.aspx.

Enterprise Risk Management & ERM. Source PwC 2020 Enterprise risk management and business continuity management: Together at last. (Accessed on 29 April, 2021). https://www.pwc.com/us/en/risk-assurance-services/publications/assets/pwc-erm-and-bcm-together-at-last.pdf.

ISO 22301: 2019 'Security and resilience — Business continuity management systems — Requirements'.

ISO 22313: 2020 'Security and resilience — Business continuity management systems — Guidance on the use of ISO 22301'.

ISO 22316: 2017 'Security and resilience — Organizational resilience — Principles and attributes'.

ISO 22319: 2017 'Security and resilience — Community resilience — Guidelines for planning the involvement of spontaneous volunteers'.

ISO 22320: 2018 'Security and resilience — Emergency management — Guidelines for incident management'.

ISO 22395: 2018 'Security and resilience — Community resilience — Guidelines for supporting vulnerable persons in an emergency'.

PD ISO/TS 22318: 2015 'Societal security — Business continuity management systems — Guidelines for supply chain continuity'.

PD ISO/TS 22330: 2018 'Security and resilience — Business continuity management systems — Guidelines for people aspects of business continuity'.

The Guardian. Department of Health writes off £9bn spent in England's Covid PPE drive. (1 February, 2022). https://www.theguardian.com/politics/2022/feb/01/department-of-health-writes-off-9bn-spent-in-uk-covid-ppe-drive.

Wikipedia entry on VUCA. https://en.wikipedia.org/wiki/Volatility,_uncertainty,_complexity_and_ambiguity.

Chapter 6

Ana Caroline Tavares da Silva, Arthur Machado Braga, Giulia Grassa Lima, Hadassa Marques de Lima, Isadora dos Santos Picolotto, Isadora dos Santos Picolotto, and Thiago de Andrade Guedes. (January, 2020). 3 Scenarios for the COVID-19 pandemic in 2021 and How to plan the future of your company when the quarantine ends?. https://www.researchgate.net/publication/346107774_3_

Scenarios_for_the_Covid-19_pandemic_in_2021_How_to_plan_the_future_of_your_company_when_the_quarantine_ends.

Charlotte Insinger on cover of 'The Future of Supervision 6' (August, 2015). https://www2.deloitte.com/content/dam/Deloitte/global/Documents/Risk/gx-cm-future-of-supervision.pdf.

COVID-19: Implications for business. McKinsey. https://www.mckinsey.com/business-functions/risk-and-resilience/our-insights/covid-19-implications-for-business.

Jacob Middeldorp. (August, 2015). The Future f Supervision 6. Deloitte. https://www2.deloitte.com/content/dam/Deloitte/global/Documents/Risk/gx-cm-future-of-supervision.pdf.

Joseph Amankwah-Amoah, Zaheer Khan, and Geoffrey Wood. (September, 2020). COVID-19 and business failures: The paradoxes of experience, scale, and scope for theory and practice. *European Management Journal*. https://www.ncbi.nlm.nih.gov/pmc/articles/PMC7474582/.

Kristin Rivera and Dave Stainback. Five ingredients to turn a corporate crisis into an opportunity; How to emerge stronger. PwC. (Accessed on 22 February, 2022). https://www.pwc.com/gx/en/issues/crisis-solutions/corporate-crisis-into-opportunity.html.

Nassim Nicholas Taleb. (2012). *Anti-fragile: Things that Gain from Disorder*. Penguin & Random House. London.

Peter Bommel. (August, 2015). The Future of Supervision 6. Deloitte. https://www2.deloitte.com/content/dam/Deloitte/global/Documents/Risk/gx-cm-future-of-supervision.pdf.

Rita Clifton, Eva Lindholm, Maryam Meddin, and Rupal Patel. (November 2020). How to emerge stronger from crisis. *Harper's Bazaar*. https://www.harpersbazaar.com/uk/people-parties/bazaar-at-work/a34698993/how-to-emerge-stronger-from-crisis/.

Sapana Agrawal, Aaron De Smet, Sébastien Lacroix, and Angelika Reich. (May, 2020). To emerge stronger from the COVID-19 crisis, companies should start reskilling their workforces now. McKinsey. https://www.mckinsey.com/business-functions/people-and-organizational-performance/our-insights/to-emerge-stronger-from-the-COVID-19-crisis-companies-should-start-reskilling-their-workforces-now.

Wikipedia reproduced definition of 'New Normal' from an article in World Economic Forum (Accessed on 5 May, 2021).

Willem Stevens. (August, 2015). The Future of Supervision 6. Deloitte. https://www2.deloitte.com/content/dam/Deloitte/global/Documents/Risk/gx-cm-future-of-supervision.pdf.

Chapter 7

Atkins *et al.* (2011). Roads to ruin study report from the Cass Business School. https://www.airmic.com/sites/default/files/technical-documents/Roads-to-Ruin-the-analysis.pdf.

Davia Temin. (8 October, 2014) .The role of boards in crisis: 10 steps for directors before, during and after Crisis. Forbes. https://www.forbes.com/sites/daviatemin/2014/10/08/the-role-of-boards-in-crisis-10-steps-for-directors-before-during-and-after-crisis/?sh=6370a4832ba4.

Deloitte's Layer Model, Deloitte. https://www2.deloitte.com/content/dam/Deloitte/uk/Documents/infrastructure-and-capital-projects/deloitte-uk-delivery-remodelled-ukversion.pdf.

Global Crisis Survey. (2021). PwC. https://www.pwc.com/gx/en/issues/crisis-solutions/global-crisis-survey.html.

ISO 9001:2008 'Quality management systems — Requirements'.

Paul DeNicola. (21 April, 2021). The crisis management crisis — and how boards can overcome it. PwC https://www.pwc.com/us/en/services/governance-insights-center/blog/crisis-management-boards.html.

Peters T. (2011). A brief history of the 7-S ('McKinsey 7-S') Model. Peters Blog. https://tompeters.com/2011/03/a-brief-history-of-the-7-s-mckinsey-7-s-model/.

Sarun Charumilind, Matt Craven, Jessica Lamb, Adam Sabow, Shubham Singhal, and Matt Wilson. (15 December and 23 August, 2021). When will the COVID-19 pandemic end?. McKinsey. https://www.mckinsey.com/industries/healthcare-systems-and-services/our-insights/when-will-the-covid-19-pandemic-end.

The board's role during crisis and beyond. (23 February, 2021). McKinsey Podcast. https://www.mckinsey.com/business-functions/strategy-and-corporate-finance/our-insights/the-boards-role-during-crisis-and-beyond.

EFQM, Brussels. *The EFQM Excellence Model.* 2nd Ed. (2021). https://efqm.org/efqm-model.

The role of the board in crisis management. Financier Worldwide. (October, 2021). https://www.financierworldwide.com/the-role-of-the-board-in-crisis-management#.YhTu2OjP1hE .

Umar Tahir. (10 December, 2019). Kubler ross change curve model. *Change Management Insight.* http://changemanagementinsight.com/kubler-ross-change-curve-model/.

Chapter 8

Adam Hayes. (2 June, 2021). Enterprise Risk Management (ERM). Investopedia. https://www.investopedia.com/terms/e/enterprise-risk-management.asp.

Committee of Sponsoring Organizations (COSOs). (2004). ERM Integrated Framework.

Deloitte Global Survey: Despite increasing dependence on third-parties, organizations are still not fully equipped to manage the extended enterprise. Deloitte. (2017). https://www2.deloitte.com/ru/en/pages/about-deloitte/articles/deloitte-global-survey-organizations-not-equipped-manage-extended-enterprise.html.

Enterprise Risk Management — Integrated Framework Executive Summary, COSO (September, 2004). https://www.coso.org/documents/coso-erm-executive-summary.pdf.

Enterprise Risk Management — Integrated Framework. COSO. (2014). https://www.coso.org/Documents/COSO-ERM-Executive-Summary.pdf.

Gina Westbrook and Alison Angus. (January, 2021). Euromonitor international top 10 global consumer trends 2021. https://www.euromonitor.com/article/what-are-the-2021-top-10-global-consumer-trends.

ISO 31000: 2018 'Risk management — Guidelines'.

Megatrends. PwC https://www.pwc.co.uk/issues/megatrends.html.

Michele Wucker. (24 January, 2019). President Xi Jinping Warns of Grey Rhino Risks. https://www.wucker.com/tag/gray-rhino/.

Michele Wucker. (9 March, 2020). The top Grey Rhino risks of 2020. https://www.thegrayrhino.com/the-top-gray-rhinos-of-2020/.

Mikaela Gavas and Samuel Pleeck. (2 March, 2021). Global trends in 2021: How COVID-19 is transforming international development. Centre for Global Development. https://www.cgdev.org/publication/global-trends-2021-how-covid-transforming-international-development.

Nassim N. Taleb, Daniel G. Goldstein, and Mark W. Spitznagel. (October, 2009). The Harvard Review. https://hbr.org/2009/10/the-six-mistakes-executives-make-in-risk-management.

National Intelligence Council. (March, 2021). Global trends 2040; A more contested world. https://www.dni.gov/files/ODNI/documents/assessments/GlobalTrends_2040.pdf.

Office of the Director of US National Intelligence. (March, 2021). The COVID-19 factor: Expanding uncertainty. https://www.dni.gov/index.php/gt2040-home/summary/the-covid-factor.

President Xi Jinping of China warning of Grey Rhino Risks. (January, 2019). http://www.gov.cn/xinwen/2019-01/21/content_5359898.htm.

Shubham Singhal. (4 January, 2021). The next normal arrives: Trends that will define 2021 — and beyond. McKinsey. https://www.mckinsey.com/featured-insights/leadership/the-next-normal-arrives-trends-that-will-define-2021-and-beyond.

Tracey Brown. (December, 2021). What is risk know-how? *Significance*, 18(6), 30–35.

www.ingramcontent.com/pod-product-compliance
Lightning Source LLC
LaVergne TN
LVHW021055220926
848484LV00021B/914